THRESHOLD
EDITIONS

BORN TO FIGHT

HOW A STREET FIGHTER
LIVING ON THE EDGE BECAME
"GAMEBRED" AND FOUND SUCCESS

JORGE MASVIDAL

THRESHOLD EDITIONS
NEW YORK   LONDON   TORONTO   SYDNEY   NEW DELHI

**THRESHOLD
EDITIONS**

An Imprint of Simon & Schuster, LLC
1230 Avenue of the Americas
New York, NY 10020

First Threshold Editions hardcover edition August 2024

THRESHOLD EDITIONS and colophon are trademarks of Simon & Schuster,
LLC

Simon & Schuster: Celebrating 100 Years of Publishing in 2024

For information about special discounts for bulk purchases, please contact
Simon & Schuster Special Sales at 1-866-506-1949 or
business@simonandschuster.com.

The Simon & Schuster Speakers Bureau can bring authors to your live event. For
more information or to book an event, contact the Simon & Schuster Speakers
Bureau at 1-866-248-3049 or visit our website at www.simonspeakers.com.

Interior design by Erika R. Genova

Manufactured in the United States of America

1   3   5   7   9   10   8   6   4   2

Library of Congress Cataloging-in-Publication Data is available.

ISBN 978-1-6680-3795-9
ISBN 978-1-6680-3797-3 (ebook)

I thank God every day for the life he gave me. Without His guiding hand,
I would have been lost a long time ago. It's only through Jesus Christ and
the Holy Spirit that I found salvation and the strength to overcome
the challenges life threw my way.

To Mami and Papi, who showed me the value of hard work and never giving up.
Your unconditional love, support, and belief kept me going.

To my two beautiful children, you are my motivation, my reason for pushing
harder every single day. I hope my journey inspires you to chase your dreams fearlessly.

To the many fans who supported me along the way, from watching me fight in backyards
on YouTube to paying for fights on Pay-Per-View.

To Paulino, Mike, Dan, and everyone at American Top Team who believed in
me when others didn't. Your guidance, wisdom, and tough love shaped me into
the fighter and man I am today. I am forever grateful.

And finally, to all the fighters out there—especially those fighting for freedom.
I see you, I respect you, and I will fight alongside you.

CONTENTS

BORN TO FIGHT

CHAPTER I

BORN TO FIGHT

Everything slowed as I walked into the blur of the green, Dominican Republic jungle, ready to break free from weeks of isolation. My senses were heightened and adrenaline pumped through my veins in anticipation of the escape ahead.

It was September 2018, and I had been isolated for nearly thirteen weeks on the mountainous Samaná Peninsula in the Dominican Republic in a town called Las Terrenas. I agreed to appear on the *Survivor*-like reality show called *Exatlón Estados Unidos* after reaching a crossroads in my fighting career. But after nearly twelve months without a fight and a new clarity on my life and career, I was sick of it. When I agreed to do the show I made sure there was an exemption for me to leave for one day on October 6 for my daughter's birthday if I was still on the show. My daughter's birthday was a week away, and the show's producers refused to let me leave for a day to see her; they said I was contractually obligated to stay, ignoring their promise. I was pissed. I've never been one to like the word "no," and so I planned my escape. I changed into a new outfit: sweatpants, high socks, and a long rash guard. I tied up my hair, put on a bucket hat, and found a T-shirt to tie around my neck as a makeshift mask. I packed a bag, grabbed my machete, and headed out into the jungle. The forest had become my home that summer, so I knew how to get out. I walked toward the jungle's opening, as I had done numerous times before. This time my target was the peak of the mountain. When you got to the top, it was crazy. You chopped your way down the other side of the mountain, and it was a completely different world, just pure wilderness. Freedom.

My heart raced as I swung the machete at the trees and dense shrubs, hacking my way up the mountain, through the jungle. *Chop. Chop. Chop.* With each strike, memories from the first thirty-three years of my life flashed through my mind.

I envisioned my father at fourteen, floating on a makeshift raft, escaping communist Cuba. He was fleeing the communist regime with two other guys, risking death over the open ocean for a shot at the American Dream. I saw my four-year-old self, waking up in the middle of the night in the living room of my aunt's cramped apartment, the Miami air thick and humid. I could hear the late-night clinking of beads as my mom made necklace after necklace while sitting on the old toddler mattress thrown onto the floor of the small room. She worked into the night—after working two day jobs—making Mardi Gras necklaces to scrape together a few extra dollars so we could live a better life and maybe one day have a place of our own.

Once I reached the mountaintop, I began my descent, hacking my way down the other side toward freedom. The world around me blurred into a green chaos. I reminisced about the streets of Miami, bouncing from one shithole to another, crashing on couches, and dragging my ass through hotels and motels. I remembered feeling that itch as I walked and rode my bike through the run-down areas of the "305" (the nickname for Miami, from its area code), seeing kids just a few years older disappearing into the temptations of drugs, gangs, and violence that consumed each inner-city block around me. That could have been me. I had to avoid

2

that dark path day after day. That was a *real* fight. And I had won. This was nothing. Each swing of the machete was fueled by the thought of my kids. I had to get back to them. I had to break free from this jungle prison. I saw myself in the Octagon, back where I knew I belonged, desperate to return. The images propelled me down the mountainside.

After hours of whacking my machete through the jungle and hitchhiking away from the *Exatlón* camp, I found myself in a small, hilly neighborhood in the Dominican countryside. By then the show's security team had been alerted to my disappearance and was out in full force searching for me. Word had spread quickly. The whole neighborhood knew I was there. All these people in Las Terrenas had worked on these shows for seven or eight years. Kids were freaking out, excited to see someone from the show. Then one of the neighborhood kids warned me: "They just pulled up. You gotta hide!"

I took off running up into the hills. These small houses were made of tin walls and roofs. The boy took me to a spot at the top where I could look down on the neighborhood. I looked out, and it was like I was watching an FBI raid. I watched as eight SUVs rolled up. As I watched the security team interrogate people down below, I felt a tap on my shoulder. I turned around and an older lady looked at me in surprise. "I couldn't believe it," she said. "They told me you were up here." She rushed me into her little house and told me to hide under the bed. She was offering me tea and sugar cookies. Sweat-soaked, I crawled under the rickety bed, ate cookies, and listened through the tin walls. As I lay under the bed, I could hear the guards going from house to house, searching for me. My mind began to wander again. I imagined getting back to the streets of Miami. I thought about what I had learned during my time alone in the jungle. I was ready to get back to the UFC, back into the Octagon, my home, where blood, sweat, and years of hard work had shaped me. I needed to get back in the cage.

Two hours passed.

Then came a knock at the door. I snapped back to reality. It was one of the show's security guards, asking the lady for a glass of water. She politely went to fill him a glass, and as she did, he stepped inside the front door. "Get out," she yelled. "What are you doing?" He spoke softly, but I recognized his voice through the tin walls. It was Yousef, one of the guards I had gotten to know during my time on the show. My heart raced.

"Jorge," Yousef said. "I know you're there."

THE POWER OF KUNG FU

The first thing I remember about my life is sitting next to my dad on the bed on Saturday mornings, eating powdered donuts with a tallboy glass of milk and some chocolate chip cookies. We sat there all morning watching the kung fu movie marathon on TV.

I was four years old and a very hyperactive kid. I was always on the move, and nothing could settle me. If cartoons were on at the time, they weren't hitting. But these kung fu movies? Mesmerizing. They were the only thing that would get me to sit still and relax. I have glimpses of lying next to Papa Dukes in bed, watching the fight scenes. To this day he still watches that shit.

Come Monday, I went to day care and inevitably found myself in trouble, whether getting into a scuffle, defending my building blocks from a would-be thief, or jumping off tables, practicing the moves I'd picked up from those kung fu movies. I managed to get kicked out of four day care centers by the time I hit four, all for the same reason: fighting. A day care center would call home: "Hey, your son got into a scrap again. Can you come pick him up?" My mom would be upset. My dad would ask, "What happened? Did he hit you first? Did you kick his ass?" making Mom lose her mind.

4

My dad was my best friend, and I was his. Then one day when I was four going on five, he just disappeared. My mom said he was in the Army. "He can't be here because he's traveling a lot. He'll be back, though," she told me. "He's very decorated." That's all I knew. We talked on the phone sometimes and he sent me a $20 roll of quarters on my birthday. But for the next nine years I didn't see him. My friends would ask about my dad sometimes. "He's in the Army," I'd tell them proudly. "What's his rank?" they'd ask. "He's, like, high up there, bro," I'd say.

For most of my formidable years, it was just me and Mama Dukes.

My mom was a machine, always hustling. She worked full-time at Dollar Car Rental, but she never settled for just one job. For as long as I can remember, she has always been into cardio, so after she worked a full day at Dollar, she spent another two or three hours teaching classes at Bally Total Fitness. She had crazy hours, but she pulled it off. I knew because when I was too young to stay home alone, I often tagged along with her to the gym. They had a day care center there, so while she was busy working, I ran around causing my own kind of havoc.

She was always coming home with a different uniform. One day it'd be black pants and some weird shit hanging around her neck. "I thought you were gonna go work the Dollar Car stuff today?" I'd ask. Dollar had an all-blue uniform with a little blazer and a skirt, and Bally had red shirts, so I knew she had picked up another gig. "No," she'd say, "I was working the catering." She was working all sorts of jobs, busting her ass. Then, late at night, while I was sleeping on the couch, she sat on the floor on the old mattress and made those bead necklaces.

It wasn't very long after Mama Dukes told me my dad left for the military when she dropped another bomb on me. "Hey," she said one day, "we're gonna go to Peru to visit your grandparents." *What are fucking grandparents?* I thought. Then it hit me. *Oh, yeah, that's right. I've met my dad's parents. I guess my mom has parents too that I haven't met. Let's go!*

We landed in Miraflores, Peru, and let me tell you, I had the time of my life. I'll never forget the first moment I saw my grandpa when we got off the airplane. "Come here!" he said. He scooped me up and sat me on his lap in the driver's seat of his car. Before I knew it, I was driving a car in another country. Me, a four-year-old about to turn five, with my hands on the steering wheel, looking at my mom like *You never let me do this. I love these guys!* It was a rush. We drove to their house and, damn, it was a nice-ass place. It was so different from what I was used to. Before my dad left, times were tough back in Miami. We were always bouncing around from shacks to apartments, crashing at people's places, sleeping in someone's garage, or checking into shitty motels. It was fun because I was with my mom but shitty at the same time. We'd stay in a motel and I didn't know why we were there. It wasn't like we were next to the beach. But in Peru my grandparents were living the good life. They had a two-story house. It blew my mind.

Peru was a complete 180 from the home I knew in Miami, with its crib mattress on the floor. It was a third-world country, but my grandparents were doing all right economically. My grandpa had been a pilot for the Peruvian air force and then became a commercial pilot. Their lifestyle was on another level. I couldn't believe my eyes. *What the fuck?* I thought. *This is our family and they have all these fucking nice things.* It was the best time of my life, but I was also kind of mad. Why didn't we live here? My grandma spoiled me rotten. Whatever I asked for, she made it happen. They let me eat candy and drink soda all day. It was a dream come true. Life couldn't have been sweeter. It was like a never-ending holiday—until it wasn't.

GROWING PAINS

I stared into the bathroom mirror of my grandparents' fancy house in Peru, tears streaming down my face. The weight of my emotions was crushing me. I felt like shit. I hadn't seen my mom in a while, and where the hell was my dad? The nights were the worst. I would lie in bed, tears soaking my pillow, crying myself to sleep night after night. This had gone on for weeks, but on that day, as I looked at my tearstained reflection, something snapped. I made a promise, one that I intended to keep. "I'm never gonna cry again," I told my five-year-old reflection.

Little did I know that that moment would be the beginning of a journey that would test my resolve in ways I couldn't imagine.

One day, a week or two after we landed in Peru, my mom started packing our bags. "Wait, you didn't pack this toy," I shouted at her. "And this one too! You forgot all these toys!" I was only five years old, but I remember that conversation like it was yesterday. When we arrived at the airport, I started hugging and kissing my grandpa goodbye. I told him how much I loved him and that I'd be back soon. I looked over at my mom, and she was a mess. Tears streaming down her face, bawling. "You're gonna miss your dad?" I asked. She couldn't even speak, just crying her heart out. I hugged the three of us together.

That's when my mom sent my world into chaos. "You're staying here," she managed to say. "I couldn't tell you. You're staying. I love you." She grabbed her stuff, got out of the car, and started rushing away toward the airport entrance. *Yeah, right*, I thought. *She's playing around.* I tried to chase after her. "No, come here!" my grandpa shouted, grabbing me and holding me back. It was a fucking struggle. "My mom!" I yelled, and cried. My mom kept walking until she faded and finally disappeared into the distance. It was like a movie. That's when it hit me: *Oh my God, I can't see her anymore.* Panic set in. I was freaking out. My grandpa tried to console me, sitting me on his lap and attempting to get me to drive again. But my head was spinning. I was disoriented. "She's gonna be back," he said. He told me that my mom had to leave because she couldn't take care of me at the moment. She had to work but promised she would come to see me soon. But "soon" turned into a year that I didn't see her.

Living in Peru wasn't exactly a walk in the park either. Back home in Miami, we faced personal difficulties, but in Peru, the country was facing its struggles. There was a far-left, communist guerrilla group called Sendero Luminoso (Shining Path) that opposed the government and was constantly wreaking havoc. They would blow up power towers, leaving us without electricity for weeks. It was a constant state of chaos, making it nearly impossible to use phones or stay connected. I still remember an incident that happened when I was around seven years old. My grandma and I had been shopping at a mall, and when we got home my grandpa and the maids were watching the news on TV. A bomb had detonated at the exact spot we had been just minutes before. My grandma was frantic, realizing the close call we had experienced. "We were just there!" she shouted. "We were just there!" I, on the other hand, didn't fully grasp the gravity of the situation. To me, bombs going off seemed like a regular occurrence. It was a different kind of normal. I cherished a lot of moments in Peru, but it was another reminder of what made America great and what could happen when a country allowed communists to gain power. Another marker that would shape my worldview.

I was the wildest kid you could imagine, bursting with energy and ready to take on the world. I had a big inclination toward combat sports, but with my grandma being a traditional South American Catholic, she had reservations the first time it came up. "Are you serious?" she said. "We're gonna put him in this?" She wanted me to play soccer, which is what every other kid in Peru was doing. All of the other kids were athletic because until the sun went down they were riding their bikes, going to the skate parks, or playing soccer. The No. 1 thing was soccer, soccer, soccer. I was exposed to it numerous times, but whenever I tried to join in, it always ended in fistfights. Every single time. I didn't know how to play, and my frustration would boil over. All I knew were Bruce Lee movies, so I would kick another kid's legs out from under them to try to get the ball away. They'd shove me. *What the hell is wrong?* I'd wonder. The second time they shoved me it was, like, *That's it, we're scrapping.* Kids would taunt me, and I would retaliate with my fists. I've been like that for as long as I can remember.

There was always a deep-rooted anger within me, fueled by the absence of my parents, the instability of my life, and the constant bullying. It was as if I was always looking for someone to take my anger out on, to fight back against the world that seemed so determined to keep me down. I know now that I was looking for someone. I didn't have my mom. I didn't have my dad. I was in another country. I was a foreigner who couldn't play soccer and spoke broken Spanish that sounded funny. Behind that anger was a desire for connection, for belonging. But in that moment all I got was in trouble. Despite the challenges, my grandma was my guiding light. She was amazing. She understood the pain I carried within me. My grandpa was in the military and he was way stricter. When I started getting kicked out of day care centers in Peru, he wanted to put me in military school. There was a fight with my mom on the phone. "No, I'm gonna pick him up any day now," she told my grandpa. "Don't do that." They put me in a preparatory school for young kids instead. I didn't last long there either.

Finally, when I was in elementary school, my grandparents relented and decided to put me in karate. I was ecstatic, convinced that finally I would learn how to fight and have the chance to prove myself. Little did I know that real karate was a whole different ball game. I had seen the movies on the bed with my dad when I was four. I thought they were going to teach me to fight and then I was going to get to do it. Peru had a significant Japanese population, the second-largest in South America after Brazil. The teacher was Japanese and was big on the fundamentals. The classes focused heavily on practicing katas, those air movements and sequences that seemed far removed from actual combat. I couldn't help but think, *Man, this isn't fighting. I want to fight.* The boredom of endless katas led to more trouble. When the instructor turned his back, I would mess around with another kid real quick and get into a sparring session, throwing punches and kicks with whatever technique I had. The teacher would catch me and whack me with a wooden stick.

I needed more than just katas and reprimands. I needed someone who would tell me, *You're practicing for a reason. I'm making you strong so that one day you can use your skills in a real fight.* But all I got were endless repetitions and long poses. Holding a pose for twenty seconds wouldn't save me in a fight; it would get me killed. Even at seven years old I thought that it was all bullshit. They finally took us to karate competitions. *Oh, it's my time to shine*, I thought. I was bummed when I found out the fights were controlled. We could hit hard and fast, but we couldn't actually hurt each other. We had to stop our strikes just shy of causing real damage and then pull back. It went against every instinct within me. I was seeing red, just trying to punch someone in the fucking face, strike them in the stomach, or kick them in the ribs as hard as I could. I didn't have that control. I got disqualified a lot. I was a misfit.

Trouble seemed to follow me like a shadow. I would get in trouble at school, and my grandma would respond by taking me off all the extracurricular activities. She believed it was contributing to my disruptive behavior, but what she didn't understand was that those activities were my outlet. Even though I wasn't good at it yet, karate allowed me to release pent-up energy and anger. You never would assume that I could fight. I was small, skinny, and quiet—traits that other kids saw as weaknesses. But beneath that quiet surface, I was angry. I got picked on and picked on and picked on. I finally realized if somebody picked on me I had to fucking address it no matter how big or mean they looked. An eleven-year-old might not sound intimidating now, but when you're only eight or nine, you think, *Fuck, this kid's big. He's gonna hurt me.* But I couldn't let myself be pushed around. Sometimes I was in a bad mood and I was just looking for somebody to take it out on. If anyone dared to fuck with me, I would fuck them up. The constant bullying and my struggles fueled my defiance. It was a survival instinct: fight back or be swallowed up.

That experience in Peru, where I confronted loneliness and violence, became my training ground for life. As I looked at myself bawling in the mirror, I realized that I couldn't go on like that, drowning in my tears. It was a turning point, the first step in hardening my heart and preparing myself for the harsh realities of the world. I was only five years old when I reached that breaking point, realizing that living in a constant state of sadness was unbearable. It was then that I made the promise to myself: *I'm not gonna cry no more. It's not bringing her back.* My dad was also absent, traveling the world with the military, as far as I knew. His sporadic calls only deepened my disappointment. I remember one call when I was in Peru and I was so excited to talk to him only for the line to cut out midway through. It was like I had lost both my mom and dad. I felt abandoned, and anger began to replace the sadness. I knew that I had to toughen up to survive.

I made a conscious choice to suppress my emotions, to build a protective barrier against the hardships that life threw at me. I didn't cry for a long-ass time after that. And so, with tears a distant memory, I pushed forward, determined to carve out my place in the world, one fight at a time.

CHAPTER 2

FIRST FIGHTS

One random night, after nearly a full year back in Miami, my mom showed up again in Peru for the first time. She never gave me any heads-up, never told me she was coming. She just appeared out of nowhere.

Mama Dukes had been back home in Miami working. So even then I always knew that there was something about America that made everybody want to go there. I wanted to go back. I didn't know it then, but the reason I was in Peru with my grandparents and my mom was back in Miami was because she couldn't support the two of us with Papa Dukes gone. My mom would call when she could, but because of the chaos in Peru we sometimes went awhile without talking. And then I wouldn't hear from her for some time.

One night in December, shortly after I had turned six, I woke up in the middle of the night, still in a haze from my dream. Standing in front of me was Mama Dukes. I rubbed my eyes and tried to go back to sleep, certain I was still dreaming. But, no, there she was. She whispered into my ear. "I'm here," she said. "I'm here." It was one or two in the morning, and I couldn't believe it. She hadn't mentioned a thing about coming. As crazy as my mom was, she knew how to surprise me, because she didn't know herself when she was coming or going. Across the room was a closet full of presents. It was one of the best Christmases ever.

My mom's visits were sporadic. Flights were expensive, and our financial situation wasn't the best. She mostly stayed in Miami, working hard to provide for us, hoping for a better life. I didn't fully understand our situation at such a young age, and nobody was telling me much.

When I was about to turn nine, after spending four years in Peru with my grandparents, my mom called and told me that I was going to leave soon and return to Miami to live with her. I had seen her only a handful of times in those years and now she was telling me I was going back home. Fuck, it was a lot to process for a kid.

It was a weird feeling to say goodbye to my grandma and grandpa. They put me on a plane and the stewardess looked after me. The flight from Peru to Miami was a blur. Suddenly I was back home with my mom in a little two-bedroom apartment she had managed to rent. It might not have been much, but it was ours. I had my own bedroom; there was a little balcony, a kitchen, and a living room. It was beautiful. That apartment on the top floor of a five-story pink apartment complex became my sanctuary, a little piece of stability in a chaotic world.

As great as it was to have our own space, I didn't know how long we'd be able to call that place home. Ever since I can remember, I had this constant traumatizing thought: *Where are we gonna live?* But in that apartment, months turned into years. From the ages of nine to thirteen, we lived in that one spot. It was the most stability I ever had growing up.

I noticed that we were considerably more broke than a lot of the other kids I went to school with, even other immigrants who had just gotten to Miami. So from my early childhood, I had this appetite for wanting to get money no matter what. Back then, money was the driving force behind everything. I didn't give a damn about Air Jordan shoes, watches, or fancy jewelry. If you saw me, I was wearing shoes from three years ago and clothes that didn't even match. None of that shit mattered to me. That's why I was always an easy target for people to pick on or talk shit about. But I didn't care. I was always in my head thinking about fighting or getting money for me and my mom. I didn't have time for small talk or caring about someone's day.

"How are you doing?" someone would ask me. *Do I fucking know you or something?* I thought. *Are you gonna give me money?* I wouldn't say it, but that was my attitude.

The neighborhood was rough, filled with a lot of immigrants from South America who had recently arrived in Miami. Many of them came from challenging backgrounds and settled in one of the lower-income areas of Miami. As a result, there was a significant presence of gang activity and drug problems. But I was just a kid, so I wasn't involved in any of that shit. My troubles mainly revolved around school, where trouble followed me from Peru to Miami.

When I came back to Miami, I felt like a fish out of water. I didn't fit in over there in Peru, and when I came back I didn't fit in in Miami either. I was a quiet, skinny little kid with a big fucking head and I didn't speak any English. Kids always took that quietness as a weak sign and assumed because I was new and kept to myself that I was weak. But I had my own thoughts I was trying to figure out. I got into a lot of altercations. I would see a kid throwing paper and I remember thinking, *I hope he hits me with it so I can fuck him up.* No one had any fucking clue that, deep down, I was praying for trouble so I could unleash my wrath on them. The paper would hit me. Bop! Just like that, I was in the principal's office. Part of me just loved fighting, and the other part was, like, *I'm in a bad fucking mood and I'm hungry.* Hunger was a big thing back then. I didn't always have food when I wanted it. I've had a massive appetite since I was a little kid, and sometimes there just wasn't any food at home. So all these things had me constantly on edge, ready for war.

So much of my life felt out of my hands. When I was young, some things were beyond my control, like whether or not we'd have dinner for the night. But as I got into grade school there was a power shift: I decided I had to take control. If we didn't have any food, I either went to a friend's house and had a meal there or resorted to a risky move like a dine-and-dash. I'm not proud of it, but a few times I went to IHOP or Denny's, sat down, placed an order, and then casually walked out. If they chased after me, I sprinted home. No one could catch me. I was running or on the bike every day.

Taking matters into my own hands became a crucial turning point. When my mom went grocery shopping at Publix, they had a stand dedicated to candy, where shoppers could fill a little bag for, like, twenty-nine cents. While my mom was shopping, I grabbed a bag and filled it up with candy. I would ask my mom to buy it, and when she wouldn't buy it, I stole it. The next day I took the bag to school and started selling the candy. That led to selling fireworks in school. They were the legal ones we could buy from roadside tents—nothing crazy. My mom would go buy some fireworks and I tried to steal a few extras, or I'd tag along with my friends on my bike and as they bought some we tried to snag a few more. One of the many times the school called my mom during my childhood was when I got caught selling the fireworks. They brought her in and explained what had happened.

I joke that my quick reflexes come from dodging my mom's blows. Every time I got in trouble, she yelled and cried and bopped me. "That's how you've been getting the extra money," she said on the way home. Around that time, when we'd go somewhere, I bought this or that or gave my mom a random $20. "It all makes sense now," she said. "But don't keep doing this."

MY FIRST FIGHT

I was in second grade when I was in my first true fight. I was nine years old, going on ten, and my friend and I were riding our bikes when we bumped into a group of older kids, maybe twelve or fourteen, along the fence near the school. "Hey, let me ask you a question," one of them shouted at me. I'm, like, "Huh?" He goes, "Get a little closer." When I rolled my bike a little closer to the fence, he stuck his hand through the fence, grabbed my shirt to pull me closer, took out a knife and said, "Get off the bike!" That's when I learned a lesson that stuck with me: never trust a stranger. Stranger danger. Don't try to be too nice. After that day, whenever somebody would enter my personal space, my sensors would go off. It happened so much around that time—I struggled to trust any-body. I slammed on the fence as hard as I could, got off my bike, and he stood on the other side laughing and pointing. "You little pussy," he said, laughing with his friends. I got back on the bike, glared at him, and rode away pissed. Shit like this happened in Peru too. These kids just wanted to mess with me and steal my bike if I left it. I got home crying because I was so pissed. This shit couldn't keep happening to me.

After lunch at school a little while later we were gathered in the court-yard, waiting for the teacher to line us up to go back to class, when all of a sudden my little friend Fernando, who was the smallest kid in class, came up crying, saying some kid slapped him. "What? Who slapped you?" I asked. He pointed over and the kid was walking away. I walked over, grabbed the kid's shoulder from behind, and as he turned toward me he instinctively slapped the fuck outta me. As his hand hit my face, I saw this was the same kid who had pulled the knife on me! I felt this immediate rage, like someone could've hit me with a bat and it would break. That's how I knew I had something extra. He was two grades older but I fucking clocked him hard—*pow! pow! pow!*—just fucking wrecked him. The PE teachers broke us up. He was already gushing blood. Not a mark on me.

17

The kid was an immigrant from Venezuela, and as we sat outside the principal's office, he started telling me how he had lost his dad and mom. I started feeling bad for the kid now. I had hated the kid and then I was, like, *Fuck, man, I'm in the same boat.* Before I could remind him that he had pulled a knife on me, they brought him to see the principal. He had been apologizing and I figured we weren't going to snitch on each other. When I walked into the principal's office, this little shit had told the principal that I attacked him, pulled a knife on him, and other bullshit. The principal was livid and called me in, ready to lay into me. "I didn't!" I told him. I was nine years old, so I didn't know how to defend myself. I felt betrayed. I learned an important lesson that day. Whether you're right or wrong, get your story out fast. Don't trust anybody. I also realized how sympathetic I could be. While still feeling angry, I felt for him missing his parents. But that rage returned when he lied. The principal was this old-school Cuban guy. Fighting was no big deal to him. He looked at me and said, "You're telling me you didn't pull a knife on him?" I was adamant. "He's the one who pulled a knife on me," I said. We were going back and forth. "Whoever pulled a knife on who, fighting is cool, but knives are not," he said. "Don't ever pull a knife." He left us with that lesson and then sent us home.

Whenever I got in trouble, my mom would take away my karate, kung fu, or boxing classes just like my grandma had in Peru. I understand why she did that. I mean, she saw that I was an aggressive kid, so why make me even more aggressive? But she also didn't understand that she was taking away my outlet. So when she took martial arts away, it backfired. I'd get even more irritated. *Oh, man, if somebody steps on my shoes, I'm gonna fucking beat their ass.* I tried my best to behave in school. I wasn't always successful, but when I managed to stay out of trouble, my mom would let me join one of those fighting classes. And as soon as I fucked up, *boom*, she'd take me out. I joined a karate school, and within three months I was one of the better kids there. But then I got in trouble at school, and I didn't see the gym for five or six months. These months away from class, that's when I found an entirely new world of fighting.

THE RIDE OF MY LIFE

Since I was a kid, I was always on the move, riding my bike on the way to somewhere. Maybe that's why I was so skinny. For as long as I can remember, my life has been all about hitting the road, going somewhere other than home—on a bike, borrowing cars, getting rides, or catching the bus. It didn't matter how I got there. I did anything just to get to the gym or a buddy's place. In the rain or blistering Miami heat, I didn't care. My bike was my ticket to freedom.

While Mama Dukes was busting her ass to make ends meet, before we moved into the top floor of that apartment building, we were constantly moving around from apartment to apartment, sleeping on somebody's couch, or going from hotels to motels, always uncomfortable. The road was my home. As an adult, I was able to identify the effects this kind of lifestyle had on me: anxiety and depressive episodes. But when I was little? I was just looking for an escape. So I was always on the move to do something else, somewhere else.

By the time I was eleven, when my mom and I finally had our own space, I made some friends in the neighborhood, including Tomas. He was my age and his family's apartment was a short ten-minute bike ride away. I'll never forget riding over to Tomas's place one Friday night. When I stepped into his place, I swear to you, it was like déjà vu. It was almost like a copy of our crib. Those Miami apartments back then all kind of looked the same. We were sitting in the living room when Tomas's fourteen-year-old brother switched something on the TV. They had one of those illegal television boxes that could stream pay-per-view channels.

"Have you guys ever seen this shit?" he asked us.

The UFC was established on my birthday when I was nine years old, but I had never heard of it until Tomas's older brother flicked it on two years later. When we saw it, we were amazed. "What the fuck is this?" I asked.

I'd seen my family gather around the TV to watch boxing when I was little, but I didn't really understand it. To me, it was just a bunch of dudes beating the crap out of each other in the ring. I couldn't understand why everyone was so excited. I remember being around seven or eight, stumbling upon boxing again, and I fell in love with it. There was no other sport that captured my attention like that. Boxing was my first love. It wasn't money that attracted me to it. I was never thinking I could make money fighting. I didn't really know what money was yet. I just knew about boxing. I watched boxing on the Latin channels whenever I got the chance, but I was still a kid, so it wasn't like I knew what fight was coming up, and we didn't have access to pay-per-view. Boxing was the only sport that I could understand, relate to and love. If it weren't for MMA, I probably would have been a boxer.

But this UFC shit, it was a whole new level. It was the greatest thing. It was everything. Don't get me wrong: boxing was cool, but it was just two dudes throwing punches. How would a boxer do against a tae kwon do guy? How would he do against a jujitsu guy? Back then those questions weren't answered until the UFC came around in 1993. Then you saw exactly what would happen to the best of the best boxers, the Tysons of the world. They'd get mopped up. These mixed martial arts (MMA) guys would scoop you up, put you on your head—and you can't throw a punch from there. The greatest boxer in the world would get their ass beat to death fighting mixed martial arts. That realization right there turned me off boxing. What would be the point of being the greatest boxer in the world? These UFC guys would beat my ass. I didn't want to be the best boxer or the best wrestler. No, I wanted to be the best *fighter* in the world, period.

Our eyes were glued to the TV when all of a sudden here came this guy that, in comparison to everybody else, looked like a stick. He weighed like 180 pounds, he was six-foot, and he was wearing some stupid-ass karate suit. I was thinking, *What the fuck is this karate gonna do? These guys are gonna kill him, bro.* There are these Muay Thai fighters, all sorts of badasses. But this skinny Brazilian guy, Royce Gracie, choked everybody out. Arm bars, chokes, you name it. *Tap! Tap! Tap!* He just ran through the whole tournament. Gracie won three of the first four UFC tournaments from 1993 to 1994. Turns out, he and his family had gotten some Hollywood producers together and made the whole UFC thing happen. They had this crazy idea to pit all styles against each other and crown one champion. One style that would reign supreme, whether it was wrestling, boxing, or whatever the hell else. The moment I saw it I thought it was the coolest thing on earth. Boxing may have been my first love, but MMA is what I wanted to do. I loved it. I understood it right away. When I watched a baseball game or a basketball game or a football game, I didn't have a fucking clue what was happening. I couldn't figure that shit out, nor did I care to. They were like foreign languages to me. But fighting—fighting was a universal language that I understood. Fighting spoke to me. It was the only thing that mattered to me. I started going to Tomas's to watch other fights and eventually rented tapes from Blockbuster Video to watch at home. I would sit there, silent and paralyzed, watching fight after fight, hour after hour. I was hooked.

Back then, money wasn't a huge motivator for me. I just knew we were broke. But I remember seeing something about the tournament winner getting something like $75,000. At eleven years old, it was mind-blowing. I could fight and make money? It was, like, *You're rich! Holy shit. Man, if I win like two tournaments that's, like, $150,000! Me and my mom, we'll be rich!*

That night ignited a fire within me, and it grew into an obsession. I didn't just want to be rich. I wanted to be the best, the baddest fighter on the planet.

JUST LIKE DAD

It was only a matter of time before the school system had enough of my shit and decided to kick my ass out. I never fit into the mold of a model student. My time at Charles R. Hadley Elementary School was a testament to that. Those poor teachers and principals had to deal with my relentless shit day in and day out. Looking back, they deserve a Nobel Peace Prize or something for putting up with me all those years. I was a troublemaker through and through. I was like a rebel without a cause. It manifested in various ways. I'd skip classes like it was a game, starting from as early as third or fourth grade. In the lunchroom, I'd do stupid shit just to stir up trouble, like throwing the leftover food from my tray in the air, causing a mess and chaos for no reason.

The fateful day came during summer school between fifth and sixth grade. Each day a bus would pick the summer school students up at the elementary and drive us over to another school for classes. To make some extra cash, I'd sell chocolates to the other kids. One Thursday I noticed $10 was missing. Someone told me they saw a particular kid take it, so I confronted him and demanded an explanation. He acted tough. "You're not gonna do shit about it," he said, unfazed. "You took my money!" I said. I told him I'd fuck him up when we got to the other school. As soon as we got there, I punched him in the face and dropped him. He admitted one of his friends took the money and promised they'd pay me back. Instead, he went and told on me and the next Monday three teachers were waiting for me when I arrived. They called my mom. "Listen, we went through hell for your boy," the assistant principal told her. "We can't handle it. Your boy is too much." They finally had had enough of me. I had two weeks until I graduated middle school and they kicked my ass out. All over $10. That was the longest time I spent at one school. I made it from kindergarten through fifth grade there, counting my repeat of first grade. I never lasted more than two or three years anywhere after that.

To make matters worse, I hadn't just been kicked out of Charles R. Hadley Elementary School; I'd been booted from the entire Dade County public school system. The principal told my mom that if I stayed in the public school system, I'd have to go to one of those alternative schools, where I'd be around other delinquents and spiral into more trouble. "If I were you," he said, "I'd put him in a private school." My mom was beside herself. "What?" she said. "We can't afford that!"

My mom was quiet the rest of the day but I could tell she was upset. That night, as we sat in the car outside of my aunt's apartment, rain pouring on the windshield, she let it out. She started crying, hitting me with her flailing arms.

"You motherfucker!" she screamed.

I tried my best to dodge her blows.

"It's gonna be all right," I said. "It's fucking school, man."

That only made her crazier.

"It's not going to be all right," she screamed. "It's not just fucking school!"

That's when she let it slip.

"You're going to end up just like your dad!"

CHAPTER 3

MY FATHER, MY SAVIOR

"You're going to end up just like your dad!"

Those nine words hit me like fucking whiplash.

"My dad's in the Army fucking making money, traveling the world. So what?" I yelled back at my mom. "What if I end up like him?"

"No he's not," she shouted. "He's in jail!"

Silence. It felt surreal. *What did she just say?*

"My dad's been in jail this whole time?" I said. "For what?"

She began to backpedal.

"I don't want to talk about it," she said.

"I want to see him right now!" I demanded. "Where is he?"

"It's not far from here," she relented.

All the hatred and animosity that I had toward my dad all those years—everything—immediately evaporated. I hadn't seen my dad since I was four and now I was twelve. I had always resented him, thinking he was this badass soldier in the Army, while my mom busted her ass trying to provide for us and we didn't have shit. All I knew about the Army was what I saw in movies. And I assumed Army members made good money. So why the fuck wasn't he helping us out?

Every year, on my birthday, he'd send me that $20 in quarters, always in rolls. My mom was struggling to make ends meet, and here was my dad, supposedly a tough guy in the Army, who couldn't even send us some real fucking money. On the few occasions he called, I treated him like shit. "We're broke. Mom has three jobs," I'd say. "You're in the Army and you can't even send us money? What are you doing for us? Don't even call me, bro."

Now it all made sense. When I was younger, some relatives had hinted at the truth. They told me I was being lied to, but I was too young to grasp or understand it. My mom didn't want to tell me the truth—that my dad was a delinquent. She didn't want me to think that would be my path too. *My dad's in jail, so I'm gonna end up in jail too.* Mama Dukes had protected me from this truth for so long, but I needed to see him. My only memory was those Saturday movie marathons with powdered donuts. It had been eight long years. I needed to know who he really was.

Meeting Papa Dukes in prison for the first time was a surreal and emotional experience. I was thirteen years old by the time we finally went through the long process of seeing him. It turned out the federal prison my dad was locked up in was just a ten-minute bike ride from our new house, which we moved into after Hurricane Andrew. I could have ridden my bike to see him.

I was nervous the first time my mom took me to the federal prison. I didn't know anything about what it was going to be like and she didn't know either. She hadn't seen him for a long time. The guards were all federal dudes, and most of them were dicks. The language barrier made it even harder. My mom didn't have great English, and my English wasn't fluent yet. It was a long procedure to get in. Visitors would sign in and sit and wait for a guard to call them up. When Mama Dukes and my turn came, we waited behind one door until they gave clearance to move to the next room. When that room filled with twenty people, they took us to the room to see the prisoners. The entire procedure was draining, and the waiting only added to the anticipation and anxiety.

The prison was a grim place, an open room filled with inmates. When I finally walked into the room to meet Papa Dukes, I was a little frozen. There he was, wearing jail khakis, shirt tucked in, cleanly shaved. My heart raced. Without hesitation, he rushed toward me and hugged me tightly. It was a surreal moment, finally meeting this guy who was supposed to be my dad after nine years but who I barely knew. All I had were stories, and most of them were wild tales from his past, where he wouldn't take a back seat to anyone and never backed away from a fight. From that first visit, we developed a close relationship. He'd call me collect almost every day, and I begged somebody to take me to go see him every week. He remained in prison for another ten years, and I treasured every moment I spent with him. My dad became my therapy, my guide, my reason for being. He was my everything. He knew me better than anybody else.

I'd see friends getting involved in shady shit, making quick money, and living flashy lifestyles. I was considering getting involved myself and mentioned to my dad how much money I could make pushing drugs. He warned me about the consequences. "You could do it, bro," he said. "You're so smart, you could actually make good money. But the moment you get caught, you're gonna fucking go crazier than anybody else. There's one thing about you since you were a kid: you always valued your freedom." He was right. Getting put in time-out was the worst thing when I was a kid. I hated being restricted, confined, or told what to do. *Damn, this guy's right*, I thought. *I don't care how broke I go. I don't want to end up here.*

So I chose a different path.

I built up the courage to share my dream with my mom and dad: I wanted to become a fighter. "This is what I want to do," I said. "I've got two choices." I presented my plan confidently, offering a backup option of joining the military just in case. My mom was hesitant about the fighting stuff, plus she thought I could use the discipline from the military. But my dad supported me wholeheartedly. "You can do anything you want to do, but that Army stuff, they're gonna be screaming in your face," he said. "I don't think you're gonna like it. You know how you are. You know how we are. I think maybe try the fighting."

Done, I thought. That's all I needed to hear.

COMING TO AMERICA

My old man's escape from Cuba when he was fourteen years old was like something out of a movie. It was 1971. He, his buddy's uncle, and one other guy had this grand plan to flee Cuba, which had become a communist hellhole. As they dreamed up their escape, they stumbled upon several inflatable tire tubes on Guanabo Beach. These tire tractor parts, which were essentially inflatable rubber tubes used inside the tires to maintain air pressure, were like gold in Cuba. They hid them away, worked tirelessly to string them together into a makeshift raft until it floated, and then they hit the high seas. All my other uncles had tried to leave before, but none of them had managed to escape. My dad got lucky and got the hell out of there.

I'd been hearing that story since I was a little kid, although I never heard it straight from my dad's mouth because he was in prison. It was like a legend passed down by the family. All the grandparents, aunts, uncles—they all talked about it. They were always talking about Cuba and politics. Every Sunday, when we got together, half the conversation was about that shit. I'd hear them complaining about "Cuba" this and "no food" that. *These fucking idiots are always complaining about*

28

something, I thought. I used to think they were just whiners and complainers. I was six or seven the first time I heard my dad's story. When I was a little older I started asking questions.

"Why would anybody get in a raft and risk their life?" I asked at the table one Sunday. "How bad was it?"

"What's your favorite color?" someone asked.

"My favorite color is red," I said.

"Over there they tell you your favorite color," they told me.

It was some mind-blowing shit. They told me that the government controlled everything. Over there, they told you what your favorite color was, what you would do for a living, and how many eggs you were allowed to eat each week. You had no choices, no freedom, nothing. And there's nothing you could do about it. If you dared to speak up against the government, they'd beat the shit out of you, put you in jail for a decade, and hope you went away. If you spoke up again they'd leave you in jail forever. In Cuba, you had to hustle for everything but you had to do things the wrong way to get ahead in life.

My father fled Cuba way ahead of anyone else in my family. The rest came much, much later. But I remember hearing this other crazy story about my dad's sister. Between Guantánamo Bay, the American base, and the nearest Cuban town, there's a field you have to get over to get to Guantánamo. The Cubans put mines in the field, so if you walked across it—*boom!*—you'd be fucking dead. My aunt, risking her life for freedom, crossed that field and a mine exploded and blew out her left tit. She almost bled out, but the guards from the embassy got her, scooped her up, brought her in, and she got to America. That was another crazy story etched in my memory. All this was engraved in me: Say no to communism.

My family has an ironic history with Fidel Castro and his communist regime. My grandfather and one of my uncles were initially seduced by Castro's promises and rhetoric, going so far as to support the regime in its early days. It didn't take long for my grandpa to see through the lies and empty promises, realizing with horror that a true communist dictatorship was being built. As he started seeing through the lies, my grandpa tried to warn other family members. "This guy's communist," he told my uncle. "We gotta back out." But by then my uncle was already deeply supporting Castro, going on missions, talking to farmers, doing crazy shit for him. When my grandpa realized they had fucked up, it was too late for my uncle. He decided to stay part of the communist party. So on one side was my grandpa and most of his kids firmly against communism. And on the other side, his oldest boy was working for Fidel. My uncle climbed the ranks fast and became an assassin for Fidel for a long time. Meanwhile, my grandpa started an anti-communist chapter of rebels, organizing strikes against the government. They planted bombs in cars at Cuban government buildings and other crazy shit. They never killed or hurt anybody, but they'd blow up power plants, knock the lights out, just trying to take down the Cuban communist regime any way they could. And now this was the topic of conversation on Sundays. I wasn't alive for all that drama, but it was the backdrop to my upbringing.

When I was young, I had mixed feelings about America. We were struggling, and it was tough as hell. We couldn't even get welfare because of my mom's immigration papers. I saw other people getting help, but not us. We were broke, and I was thinking, *What the hell is going on in this country? Everything's so damn expensive and we can't afford nothing.* When I lived in Peru, it was a different story. My grandparents were doing all right economically, so I didn't understand what was going on in America. I just knew communism was really bad. When I got older, even though my dad was in jail, he'd tell me, "This is the greatest country ever." He understood he had made a mistake. If my life was hard, his was twenty times harder. If I needed to know how great America was, all I had to do was listen again to what he had risked to make it over here. My dad's story is a testament to the greatness of America. It's a place where people like my old man come seeking a better life.

My dad is one of the craziest dudes. It takes a special kind of crazy to escape Cuba on a tractor tire raft and paddle 110 miles from Havana to South Florida. After he and the two other guys had finessed the tractor tire to make it fit for sea, they filled up a gallon drum with water and tied it to the raft. But the water tank wasn't wrapped right and got contaminated with salt water on the fourth day at sea. Then they were out at sea with no fresh water to drink. It was a nightmare. My dad and the two other guys thought it would take a day to get to Florida, but before they knew it, they were lost.

As the tractor tire floated along on the third day, my dad held up his paddle in the air and a bird, a seagull or something, landed on it. He started lowering it, thinking, *Man it's been three days, I'll just eat this bird.*

"Maybe we should eat this," he told the other two guys.

"Hey, don't do that," the guy next to him said. "It's a sign from God we're gonna make it."

My dad shook the paddle, the bird flew off, and they started paddling again. Some time passed and when my dad got tired again he sat back with the paddle up. The bird came back. He started lowering his paddle.

"We're eating it," he said.

"I told you, man," one of the others said, "it's a sign."

"You're right," my dad said. "It's a sign from God . . . to eat!"

"You ate it?" I asked him years later.

"Yeah, I was so damn thirsty, I drank the blood," he said. "I bit right into that raw meat." That's fucking survival.

Seven days after they set sail from Cuba, my dad's tractor tire raft washed up in the Bahamas. From there, he got extradited to Miami all by himself at the age of fourteen. That's where his journey in America began. He was an immigrant with no other family or friends there, so the government sent him to the ghetto projects in Liberty City, paying, like, fifty bucks a month for rent, and enrolled him in a local school. He grew up there, surrounded by people of completely different backgrounds and cultures, with nobody he could depend on: his mom and dad were still in Cuba. His aunts, uncles—everyone he knew was back there. He was the first one to make it here and he was alone in the projects, not knowing a word of English. He went to school, and he told me it was hell. He had to run through the neighborhood just to be safe because the other kids wanted to fuck him up for no reason. He was in the worst of the worst of Miami. Being Cuban made him stand out even more. After just the second day of school, he had enough. The teachers paid him no attention and none of them spoke Spanish. He hated it, so he quit.

Before my dad knew it, he met another Cuban kid who had moved to the projects too. After just a few months in Florida, they took off for California and started living the thug life. The only way my dad knew how to make money was the wrong way. My dad was a real bad guy for a while. They'd drive around Beverly Hills and look for housemaids. My dad was good-looking, so when he'd see a lady who looked like she might be a maid, he'd say, "Hey, how're you? Need a ride?" He'd give them a ride, get them to fall for him. Then he'd find out when the owners were gone from the house. The maids would say, "I can't come Wednesday: I gotta babysit." Then they'd hit the houses when nobody was there and take all the jewelry.

During one run, my dad gave some jewelry to a guy who promised to give him cash later for it. Days turned into weeks and weeks turned into months. with no word from the guy. Then he got a knock at the door. It was the guy. My dad had tried to trace him with no luck for months and now he was at the front door. "Yeah, I wasted the money. I don't have it," he said. "I'm not paying you." He pulled out a knife, trying to intimidate my dad, maybe even kill him. The dude fucked up because my dad always had a piece nearby. My dad smoked him—*pow! pow! pow!* The guy died right there. "Let's go!" my dad told the girl he was with. The place wasn't in his name. But the girl left something behind, and when she went back, guess who was waiting? The boys in blue. They broke her down and she snitched. My dad was a thug then, coming from bad neighborhoods. He didn't know better. He wasn't about to call the police and say, like, *I just smoked this dude who came here to kill me because he owed me $80K.* He might not have done any time if he had stayed, but he took off. He served five years for manslaughter in a California state prison.

After his release he made his way back to Miami and got back on his feet, going back to illegal hustles, because that's all he knew. He met my mom in Miami and started moving cocaine to make money. His whole life to that point consisted of partaking in illegal activities. In the short time I knew my dad before he got locked up, I was too young, and he shielded me from it. My only glimpse into his world came when I was four. I was in the apartment bedroom watching TV and my dad brought me snacks. "Stay in the room," he said. Papa Dukes never yelled at me, never hit me, but I was scared of him. If he looked at me, I'd crumble. I forgot I wasn't supposed to leave and went out into the living room. "What are you doing?" he screamed. "Get in the fucking room!" I remember seeing keys and a bunch of white powder. That's the only shit I ever saw.

Eventually, some of the people my dad pushed cocaine with got pinched and wore wires. It was a whole operation. He wasn't part of the sting, but they had enough dirt on him to send him away. I was about to turn five when they gave him twenty years in federal prison for drug trafficking.

My dad was gone and I was left to grow up in the residue of that environment. It wasn't an easy road, but my dad believed in the American Dream with all his heart. With time, I learned to appreciate the sacrifices my family made, the risks they took, and the opportunities they created. Papa Dukes might have had a wild and rough life, but he also taught me the importance of making the right choices and fighting for a better future.

A PIVOTAL LESSON

Despite the troubles I had in school and the fights I got into, there was something about those experiences that taught me valuable lessons about survival and resilience. Life in those times toughened me up and shaped my character. It made me realize that sometimes you have to fight to survive.

After I got kicked out of Charles R. Hadley Elementary, my mom enrolled me at Francisco Baldor, a somewhat affordable private school for three or four grand a year. Mom busted her ass to pay for it.

One of my favorite pranks was calling up Papa John's and ordering a bunch of pizzas to the school. This was back when they had phones in the school. I'd call Papa John's and they'd see the school number pop up. "Oh, Francisco Baldor! How many pizzas?" they'd asked. I would think of the nastiest pizzas that nobody was going to eat. "Miss Abigail wants ten cheese, ten anchovies . . . ," I'd say. I'd hang up and go back to class and wait. Any errand the teacher needed, I was on it.

"Anybody want to deliver the attendance?" she asked the class.

"Me! Me! Me!" I said, shooting my hand into the air. "Please! I'll come right back."

"Okay," she said. "Masvidal."

Teachers loved when I wasn't in class. I'd roam the halls and wait until I saw the pizza delivery guy pull up and go into the office.

"Miss, I got the attendance," I said.

"One second . . . ," the school secretary said, turning her attention to the delivery guy. "Nobody called from here and ordered thirty pizzas."

I giggled as the confusion and chaos unfolded. They finally caught my ass doing that, along with a few other transgressions. I pulled the fire alarm, got in fights, and skipped class. It was a mountain of shit. I lasted at Francisco Baldor for a year and change before my shit caught up with me again and I was kicked out. A few weeks before summer, I was back to the public school system at Arvida Middle School.

That summer, between sixth and seventh grade, I got into my first serious fight. Me and my boys from the neighborhood were looking for pool parties with girls, but things didn't go as planned. We went to two different parties and there were no girls. "You told me there was gonna be girls," I said. "It's fucking dudes." By then I was always training, and this was a waste of time. I was in a bad mood. As we were leaving the second party we ended up crossing paths with a big group of dudes on bikes and one of them was just staring at me for no reason. I nodded my head at him. "I don't fucking know you," he said. I dropped my bike. "What are you talking crazy for?" He got off his bike and we started going at it. The kid was my age, but he was with some older dudes who were high school dropouts, the neighborhood bullies and thugs. They were petty punks, part of a little bullshit gang. After the fight, one of these nineteen-year-old dudes walked out of the Blockbuster and saw their friend bleeding. "You did that to my boy?" one of them said to me. "Yeah, I did that to your boy," I said. Two more older guys came out and said, "What's up?" I grabbed my bike and bounced.

My friends showed up at my house later that day. They said, "Bro, these guys just showed up at my house and my dad just called me," one of my friends said. These guys didn't know where I lived, so they went to my friends to deliver the message. "They're three cars deep. They want to fuck you up." I never would run from a fight. So I went to find them along the street near the middle school. When I got there, this nineteen-year-old loser was talking shit. He was in his dropped-out minivan with gold rims near the ice-cream trucks, trying to hit on middle school girls. Someone called me over to the van: "Masvidal, come on over."

The dude who had confronted me earlier popped his head out. "I'm that dude you were talking shit to. I'm about to beat your ass right here in front of everybody."

I had just been kicked out of Baldor and didn't really have friends at Arvida. But I wasn't about to back down. "Fuck you, bro, and everybody in this fucking car!" I shouted into the van.

The dude got out of the van, ordered a steak sandwich from the ice-cream truck, and ate it, and five minutes later we were fighting. He must have been the biggest idiot ever because you can't eat before any physical activity, much less fighting.

I was five years younger, but by then I had been training since I was in Peru. I had seen the UFC at my friend's house when I was eleven, and even though I never had coaching, I saw the moves and did them with my friends when we wrestled. Compared to those street punks, it was a bad recipe. My hands and speed were nasty. I didn't hit hard but I was a volume puncher and knew some chokes. I started to beat the hell out of the guy. He threw a punch, and I ducked under, took him down, and choked him as hard as I could, squeezing for dear life with everything I had. All of a sudden his boys started kicking my head until I saw black and released him. He was spitting up blood and I stumbled to my feet, all dizzy and seeing double. My friends held me. "Bro, get the fuck out of here," they said. "There's a lot of them!"

I stumbled over to my bike, barely able to see straight. Everything was blurry. Then one of his friends, another high school dropout on steroids, also about nineteen, came up to me.

"Fucking pussy, fight *me*!" he shouted.

"I'll fight you tomorrow!" I yelled back. I got on my bike and tried to ride away from the scene. My head was spinning. I was seeing double. I wasn't trying to fight.

"Fight me," he said. He was getting closer.

"Hey, bro, back up," I said.

"You're a pussy!" he shouted again. He made that noise where you hock up the saliva in your mouth. Then he spit right on my chest.

Suddenly, everything went away: the dizziness, the pain from getting kicked in the head, all of it. *Snap.* I went into Hulk mode.

My jean shorts were loose from the earlier scrap, so I tightened my belt and immediately started going after him. He played football and I wasn't very good at wrestling, so he got under me, scooped me up, and slammed me back to the ground. But he had no idea what to do next. I'd seen a leg choke movement in UFC, so I grabbed his head with my legs, squeezed as hard as I could, and started punching him in the face. One of his friends tried kicking me but I blocked it and let the dude go. I jumped to my feet and put my hands up, and they all backed up. They wanted none of me when I was on my feet. That was when I knew I could fight no matter what. It was when I saw that there were different levels to a human being. I got on my bike. "Don't worry," I yelled, "I've got friends too!" I didn't have many at Arvida, but back in my neighborhood I knew some older kids too. Then I pedaled off to my friend's house.

I was exhausted by the time I arrived. I'd already been in two fights. Back then we only had house phones. My friend Mike's older brother, Mario, was a sophomore, but he knew a lot of people in middle school and someone had called the house. "Everybody has been blowing me up," he said. "That dude who jumped you is still there talking shit, said he kicked in your head."

I told my friend, "Bro, get your bike, we're going there right now." We both got on his bike and he towed me on the back.

When we got there, I immediately saw the guy. "Nick!" I screamed, already running at him. "Nick!" I yelled again. He turned around and *bam!*—I punched him in the fucking head. We started going at it again. This time it was on school grounds, unlike the other fights, which had taken place several blocks away.

He did a football tackle, scooped me, and slammed me on the ground. When he slammed me, I caught him in the same rear naked choke as before, but he had earrings and they ripped off, blood spewing everywhere. His friends started kicking me and I started punching him more: *Boom! Boom! Boom!* I started choking him harder and they started kicking me harder. Then I went unconscious. I was already training and competing, so I could defend myself, but not from four or five people. The teachers and security ran out of the school and broke it up. They suspended me for ten days on the spot; I was already halfway to getting expelled at my new school. They called my mom, who drove over to pick me up. "Oh my God," she screamed when she saw me. The cartilage in my ear had exploded on one side, and I was bleeding outward over the ear. My face was wrecked from the gravel. My ribs were bruised and fucked-up. It was the first time my mom didn't kick my ass for fighting. She drove me to the ER. We sat in the waiting room, my mom crying. "I can't believe they did this!" she said. I tried to reassure her. "I'm gonna be all right, Mom," I said. "This happens all the time." It was a traumatic scene. I had a nasty concussion that kept me awake, but no broken bones. Thankfully God made me out of steel.

I wanted to kill those guys. That was an ongoing thought in the days that followed. These three guys had beaten the shit out of me. I wanted to stab them. I needed to talk to my dad. A few days later, all of a sudden Papa Dukes called from prison. He was incarcerated, but it always felt like we were connected. I had been trying to talk to him about the situation, but I couldn't tell him over the phone what I wanted to do. "I have to see you in person," I told him. He told me to to visit him with my grandma and his sister the next time. I relented. "Fucking okay," I said.

The next weekend I went with my aunt and grandma. I still didn't want to say anything around them. We were close but I didn't want them hearing it. I sat there anxiously waiting for the right time. And then the visit was over. The guards warned us it was time to go. "Oh, you had something to tell me," my dad said at the last moment. I pulled him aside and briefly told him what happened. "I'm gonna hurt these guys, Dad," I said. "I'm gonna hurt them." But my dad, even from behind bars, remained a guiding force in my life. He started lecturing me. "Listen, what you're planning to do, you're going to end up in here," he said. "You can do it, but there's a big chance you're gonna end up right in here, and your freedom is gone." It was simple yet profound advice that stuck with me. I couldn't let my emotions cloud my judgment.

I kept having beefs with the same kids whenever we saw each other. One day, while riding my bike to Kmart, I saw them again, three of them, and I was all alone. Back then I was alone a lot. I got off my bike and one of them noticed me. I started walking, then running, to the sporting goods section, where I found a bat. With the bat in my hands, I acted like I was going to pay for it at the checkout. I wanted to show them that I wasn't defenseless. The guys followed me, curious to see if I would actually buy the bat. But as soon as they saw me at the checkout counter, I put the bat down and sprinted out of the store. I hopped on my bike and rode away as fast as I could, leaving them behind.

I realized I couldn't live like this. I was going to end up in the hospital with the shit beat out of me or these guys were going to fucking kill me. My dad would give me advice for protection. "You can't take a knife," he said. "If they catch you with a knife, you're gonna get in trouble." But Papa Dukes said I could take a pair of long tube socks and the padlock from my school locker, place the padlock inside one sock and put them inside the other sock, and I would have a formidable weapon of self-defense if I needed it. An extra pair of socks and a lock—can't get in trouble for those! I was, like, "Dad you're the smartest guy!"

I learned a lot every time I visited my dad. As we waited in that prison waiting room for the number of visitors to reach twenty people, I often found myself talking to other family members who were there to visit their incarcerated loved ones. "How old are you?" some lady would ask. I'd tell her and she'd tell me the story of their son or grandson getting locked up when he was my age and now he was thirty-five. "You remind me a lot of my son," the lady would say. "He was a good kid like you, and then one day . . ." The stories always ended with the son being in the wrong place at the wrong time. It was a constant reminder of how easily one wrong move could change the course of your life.

My experiences in the rough streets of Miami toughened me up, but it was my dad's wisdom that steered me away from self-destruction. I realized that my life needed a new direction. Sometimes the strongest thing you can do is walk away and choose a better path.

CHAPTER 4

STREET FIGHTING

I was having one of those days. The kind where you just say, "Fuck it," and ditch school. I had mentally checked out of school by around middle school. I had this routine: I would go to school for the free breakfast, go back to my aunt's house, where Mama Dukes and I were living at the time, and come back for lunch.

I planned to go back to school that day for lunch, but when I got to my aunt's house after breakfast, I started watching a Bruce Lee movie, *Enter the Dragon*. I was transfixed by it. I remember the underground tournament scene, where Lee's character infiltrates a secret fighting competition. Watching Lee face off against Han was a master class in martial arts. I was blown away watching Lee's speed and precision. I think everybody wanted to be a fighter after that movie, myself included. I was so inspired. I skipped the entire school day.

The tae kwon do studio was about a twenty-minute bike ride away, and after watching Bruce Lee do his thing, I hopped on my bike and pedaled like a madman. I was thinking to myself, *This is the coolest shit ever!* My mom had been busting her ass my whole life, complaining about her job, and I was, like, *I'm gonna ride my bike to this fucking place, train my ass off, ride back, and hopefully there'll be some Hot Pockets waiting for me. Then I'll do it all over again tomorrow.* That's what I wanted to do for the rest of my life. At thirteen years old, I already knew that fighting was what I wanted to do. School had given me a beatdown. It was kicking my ass every time I had to pay attention in class or do homework. I was already hitting the gym at least once a day, sometimes twice. It was just a matter of time before I dropped out.

I told my mom, "I got a way out." I kept watching UFC. Now the prize money was $100,000 for winning the tournament. Three fights in one night. I tried explaining it to my mom, but she looked at me like I was insane. "You get into a cage, and then you fight three times in one night, Mom, and then *boom*, one hundred grand!" I remember telling my mom, "Mom, when I become a big guy, I could do this." Can you imagine? Imagine this poor lady: she'd never even heard of fighting, and I couldn't even show it to her because we didn't have that pay-per-view. My poor mom was, like, *What the fuck is this kid talking about?* "What do you mean two guys fight in a cage?" she said. "No, you're gonna go to school and study." Sigh. "I'm meant to fight, Mom," I told her. "I know I'm a fighter." Plus part of me was thinking, *We're broke. I could do this for us.*

My mom thought I was batshit crazy for years. She thought I was getting these wild ideas from watching too many cartoons or something. It wasn't until I could rent the UFC fights from Blockbuster that I could finally show her. I rented one of the fight tapes on VHS and put it in the VCR. "Mom, this is what I want to do." She cried when she saw a UFC fight for the first time. I had been talking about this shit for a while, but I had never been able to show her, and it wasn't everywhere on TV. If I mentioned UFC back then, most people would be, like, *What the fuck is that? You mean KFC?* Not too many people knew about the UFC in those days. Cage? Guys fighting? It sounded barbarian.

Whenever I got in trouble at school and my mom took away my karate classes, I had to find other ways to satisfy my craving. I practiced on my own and shadowboxed, throwing punches and kicks in the air. When I was grounded, my mom would still let me go to my friends' places, so if I had a friend who liked fighting, I rode my bike over there and we put on the gloves and went at it. I was in love with the violence of taking someone out with my hands. I wasn't the strongest kid naturally, but when it came to speed and reflexes, I was off the charts. From my first fight as a little kid, I learned two things: I've got really fast hands and I'm really good at seeing the punches. But I knew I couldn't rely solely on striking. This wrestling shit and Brazilian jujitsu—I had to learn that stuff because I didn't want to get tapped out. All the UFC tournament winners had those skills.

When I was thirteen, Mama Dukes and I moved to our own house and I met some dudes four years older than me who were obsessed with UFC too. I went to their house and we watched all the UFC fights. Now I was watching the fights, mimicking the moves of the fighters. These kids were bigger and stronger, so they roughed me up, but I kept at it and eventually started to get the moves down. I was doing the finishing holds and submissions. *I want to make this official*, I thought. I did whatever I could to find a gym. Money was tight, though. The schools were charging, like, fifty bucks a week, and if you wanted to train multiple times, it added up to a hundred. That's why homework was never a thing for me. I had to get money. I offered to clean the gym and mats in exchange for training. They let me train free there for a bit, but eventually, they were, like, *You're here like four or five times a week. You need to pay.* We couldn't pay, so I had to leave to go find another gym. And so I walked into the high school wrestling room.

I'M GOING TO BE A FIGHTER

I was a scrawny fifteen-year-old kid when I stepped onto the wrestling mat for the first time to try out for the varsity team at Sunset Senior

High, with its long-running wrestling program. All these kids had been wrestling for years, and then there was me, a skinny freshman with a huge mountain to climb.

It was a bumpy road to high school. I got kicked out of not one but two more schools on my way there. Life was already throwing me some hard punches. To make matters worse, I couldn't get out of my own way. I got a taste of real wrestling in eighth grade before I got kicked out. The school that I was in at the time had a wrestling program that lasted for a few weeks before getting shut down, and from the moment I stepped onto that mat, I loved it. I had been fighting my whole damn life, and on the streets I could stick with anybody, no problem. I was quick, mean, and never afraid to throw down. But when it came to grappling and wrestling, that shit was a different story. I may not have been the strongest or most technical wrestler, but I refused to back down from anyone.

When I got to my first wrestling practice, I saw immediately that I had a chance. The kids above and below me at 140 and 154 pounds would kick my ass from Monday to Sunday because they had wrestled since they were practically toddlers. But in my 147-pound weight class, there were no returning seniors or even juniors. Everybody who was trying out for the starting spot had only been on the team for a year or two. I could beat them. The spot was up for grabs, and I took that shit seriously. I attended every practice and every training session. I started to realize that maybe I wasn't as bad at the wrestling stuff as I thought. When the season approached, the coach set up a wrestle-off and I ended up claiming the No. 1 spot at 147 pounds. It was pretty much set: I was going to be the starter as a freshman. I was on top of the world until my coach reminded me of my biggest hurdle.

"Make sure you've got your grades in check," he told me.

"What do you mean grades?" I asked.

"You have to have a 2.0 to compete in scholastic programs, Mr. Masvidal," he told me. "What are you so worried about?"

"What if my grades aren't good?" I asked. "Can I still compete?"

"No," he said, "you have to have a 2.0."

School biting me in the ass again. Hindsight is 20/20, and, looking back, I realized that there was more to it than just a lack of interest. After I moved back to America from Peru and continued getting in trouble, my mom had me tested for numerous things, and it turned out I had ADHD. The doctors wanted to prescribe medication, but my mom refused. My cousin had been on pills and my mom said it turned her into a zombie. "She's nothing like what she used to be," she said. "That's not my niece that I know. I'm not gonna do that to my son." So, natural she kept me; Mama Dukes never let me go on any medication. Maybe it was for the best, but I was always anxious around other kids and big groups. That and the anxiety caused by constantly moving from one apartment to another made it challenging to focus.

On top of that, girls were a whole different distraction. Let's say I was paying attention to whatever calculus class I was in. One minute, I would be trying to focus, and the next I'd get tapped on the shoulder with a note in the shape of a heart. "From Abby: You're cute. Do you want to get lunch?" Who even was Abby? I would turn around, see some girl waving at me, and *bam*, I'd realize that the teacher had already gone on for fifteen minutes. And let's be real: I didn't give a damn about calculus or any other class. I was more interested in making money and getting to the gym. School just didn't click for me, so I gave up. I slept through class and copied someone else's work when I woke up. Lunchtime was my reason for being at school. I could be found eating like there was no tomorrow at all the lunch periods, from first to third. I knew all my friends' codes, and if one of them wasn't eating that day I punched in my friend's code—*dah, dah, dah*—and, just like that, free lunch. There was always a side hustle.

When my report card finally came back, it showed a GPA of 1.2, nowhere near the required 2.0. "Well, it's by term," my coach said, "so if you can get your grades up for the next quarter, we'll let you wrestle then." If I could get those grades up, I'd get a shot at wrestling later in the season. Playoffs, districts, regionals, state tournament—all of that was on the table. I tried to improve my grades, I really did. But when the next report card came, the best I could do was 1.5. It hit me so hard. I felt like I was finally doing something meaningful with my life—I was going to be part of a team—and even that fell through.

Without wrestling to keep me in line, I found myself wandering back down a familiar path, skipping school and getting into trouble. It wasn't long before I found myself in a confrontation with three guys looking to pick a fight. I may have had a history of starting shit, but that time I was provoked. They came at me, expecting me to back down, but I stood my ground and fought back. I knocked one out with a punch, and the other two ran off to the security guards. "He attacked us," they told them. There weren't many cameras in the school, but where the fight went down, lucky me, there was one. The incident was on camera, and I faced a hefty ten-day suspension and another expulsion. In the Miami public school system, after twenty days of outdoor suspension a student would be kicked out, destined to a special alternative school. My mom never wanted me to go to one of those because she thought I would end up in jail.

That fight would have been the end of it if not for the assistant principal, who loved my mom. Since I was provoked, he managed to lessen the punishment to five days of suspension and advised my mom to transfer me to another high school. "He'll be in the public system if he gets kicked out," he said. "Just transfer out and start clean at another school." My mom withdrew me from Sunset and transferred me to Felix Varela Senior High School down the street.

X X X

I was fifteen and had my mind made up. School wasn't for me. I waited a couple of months, turned sixteen, the legal age to drop out, and that's exactly what I did. "I can't do this shit no more," I told my mom. "I'm gonna get to work." School was just eight hours of sleep and felt like a waste. I wanted to do something with my life, and sitting in a classroom wasn't it. Mama Dukes didn't let any time slide: she made sure I got that GED right away. It took me eight months to get that fucking thing, but I got it. She hung it on the fridge like a trophy.

But my eyes were set on something bigger. I knew I wanted to be a fighter. I remembered that UFC tournament when I was eleven years old where the winners made $75,000. The numbers had only gone up since then, and I was dead set on becoming a UFC fighter. My mind was different from other sixteen-year-olds. I was already thinking about real-life shit. I knew how to read, write, and do math in two languages. For everything else, I figured I could hire someone.

I was still two years away from being able to fight professionally, but that didn't matter. It was the perfect time to focus on honing my skills, building my amateur record, and competing. I was going to make it happen no matter what. I didn't have any other choice. I turned my entire focus to working and training my ass off.

SLEEP, EAT, TRAIN

I had more jobs than I can count after I dropped out. Seasonal jobs, one-off gigs, you name it. I couldn't get any real jobs in Miami. I just wasn't lucky. I applied everywhere: McDonald's, Burger King, Publix, Winn-Dixie. I never even came close to getting an interview. I wouldn't even get a callback. If you're from the South, you know that Publix hires practically everybody. Not even Publix gave me a job. Nobody wanted to give me a job. I kept applying and kept trying. I noticed one day, *Man, my handwriting is shit.* I got my cousin to fill out all my applications with her nice handwriting. At least that way maybe I could get an interview. That's exactly what happened, but still couldn't land a job. Something about me would throw up a red flag to the hiring manager, who must have thought, *Man, this guy's a fuck. I'm not gonna hire him.*

The summer before I turned seventeen, I visited my aunt in Sarasota, Florida, and tagged along with her to the mall one day. She was shopping her ass off and I didn't have a dollar on me, so I started wandering around. I saw a wall with notices of job openings everywhere taped up and down. The place had a hundred listings. So I started filling out applications with my bad handwriting, barely legible, and turned them in. I started getting calls almost immediately, that same day. That had never happened in Miami. In Sarasota, I was, like, the only fish in the pond. I thought, *Fuck, this is good.* Five places called me back right away, so I decided to move to Sarasota for the summer. I picked up a quick job at the mall, and from there I quickly found myself a telemarketing job. I practically stayed for free at my aunt's house and saved as much money as I could. I'd give her $100 a week and the rest would stay with me. In those ten weeks, I made, like, three grand working the telemarketing jobs and other gigs I could find.

I actually wasn't that bad at it. I got paid based on how many sales I made per hour and how many calls I made. I was shooting my shot all day long. I called the numbers on my list and the pitch went something like this: *Hey, how are you? I'm Jorge Masvidal, and I'm calling from* Timeshare *magazine. I've just entered your name into the million-dollar sweepstakes for Publishers Clearing House.* That's how I hooked them. They went, *Oh, what do you mean?* I'd say, *Your name is Stephanie Bartholomew? So there's a million-dollar sweepstakes. We just enlisted you in it and I just wanted to tell you about it. If you buy seven magazines a month, it'll only cost you $4.99. Think about how much you can read and travel from your living room all over the world.* Once they got close to agreeing, I transferred them to my supervisor. My goal was to get as many people as possible on the phone with my supervisor so they could seal the deal and get their credit card info. I shot that script out all day and night. If I wasn't at the gym, I was making calls. I worked one shift from 9 a.m. to 6 p.m. and eventually, I picked up another shift calling people who lived on the West Coast and Hawaii from 7 p.m. until 11 p.m.

Everything revolved around two things: fighting and making money. Whether it was to support my mom or invest in my training, I knew we were hurting for money. Comparing our lifestyle to everyone else's, we were far below average. Even though I was broke, from the time I was a teenager, I understood the value of a dollar, because that dollar meant the difference between going to bed hungry or being able to afford a cheeseburger at McDonald's. Back then I could get a hamburger for twenty-nine cents on a Wednesday and a cheeseburger for thirty-nine cents on a Sunday. Those were the days!

As I got closer to eighteen, I was still moving between places. At one point I found myself staying with Mama Dukes at one of her friend's houses, cramped in the living room with a small plastic closet from Walmart acting as our makeshift storage unit. When friends or family came over, it was the most awkward thing ever. I was desperate to escape. That environment fueled my anxiety and pushed me toward destructive behavior. *I can't live like this*, I thought. *I can't lay here and wait. I'm not gonna wait for nobody.*

The gym became my sanctuary, my safe place amidst the chaos. As many crazy variables that could happen in the gym, I always felt a sense of control. At least there my destiny was in my hands. I couldn't say the same at home. If I wanted to eat, there wasn't even food there. What the fuck was I going to do there? I might as well make some money, get some food, and train my ass off. So that's what I did. Every chance I got.

My aunt was married to the general manager at a prestigious Nissan and Volvo dealership in West Florida. I told him, "I need a fucking car." So he found me a car for $800, a four-door baby blue Pontiac Bonneville from 1984, the same year I was born. I bought the car, drove back to Miami, and put three months down at Freestyle Fighting Academy. That's all I needed. After three months or so the gym owner saw what a workhorse I was. I'd practice five or six hours, take a nap under the ring, go to the nearby Publix for food, sleep under the ring, teach a night class, train again, clean the mats, and sleep in my Pontiac. Eventually, they just had me clean mats for my membership. Whenever I had the time, I would take on any odd job I could find to make some extra money. I worked at a petting zoo for kids and at an event catering company as a bar helper. I still couldn't get *real* jobs in Miami.

I left rinky-dink gyms behind and found myself training at some of the top-notch places in Miami. Kung fu, karate, and tae kwon do were valuable experiences, but I knew I needed a more solid foundation with a focus on wrestling and boxing to excel in MMA. I needed something with real competition. Freestyle Fighting Academy was a game-changer. The gym attracted some serious talent, including Cuban boxers who had defected to Miami and brought their skills and expertise with them. I walked into that gym and there would be a handful of Olympians, gold medalists, silver medalists, and current world champions, all from Cuba. They drew in a mix of world-class athletes from all over, and I was there with them. That's where I started learning jujitsu and grappling.

I rotated between three gyms, each offering something slightly different. In addition to Freestyle Fighting Academy, I eventually trained at Young Tigers Foundation and American Top Team. Each gym had its unique approach, one focusing on boxing and striking; another on MMA; and the third on wrestling and traditional martial arts. It's like when you're popular in school and you get invited to the Friday night party. I wasn't that kid in school, but in the gym? I was that guy. Everyone could tell I was exceptionally talented. An older fighter would see me and go, *Wow, you're really good. What gyms do you train at?* I'd tell him and he'd invite me to another gym. The mix of training locations and styles was exactly what I needed.

Housing was an ongoing challenge, but it didn't bother me. On and off I couldn't pay rent and was without a place. I'd think, *Well, if I can't pay rent this month, I'll stay in the car.* That Pontiac fueled my unconventional lifestyle. It was all part of chasing the dream. My life revolved around training, eating, and sleeping, and my car became my home. I would park it at the gym I was going to train at the next morning, never knowing where I might spend the next night. A lot of days I would be the first guy in the gym. Guys would be, like, *You're so disciplined.* No, I literally lived there. The gyms were spread across the city. I would train at two, sometimes all three gyms each day. Whenever I didn't go to a particular gym, the coach would talk shit and tell me I was slacking. Every sixteen blocks is a mile in Miami, so that also included six miles on my bike. I fell into a routine. Mornings usually started at 9 a.m. at the wrestling gym, where I would train for two hours. Between training sessions, I'd hang my shit out to dry because I had another session and didn't have any money to buy more clothes. After a forty-five-minute lunch break, I would ride my bike three miles to the next gym for two more hours of striking practice. In the evenings I would either ride to the third gym for boxing or return to my Pontiac. It was the fighter's life. The car was comfortable enough to sleep in, but two windows didn't go down and the AC was broken, so oftentimes it was hot and muggy. But I knew it was temporary; I was going to get myself out of that place. At night I'd lay in the back seat, windows down, stars above, and envision a day when I would open the fridge and it would be filled with food and I could do whatever the hell I wanted.

I didn't care about anything but training. I knew there'd be a time and a place for a more extravagant life, but it wasn't now. When I wasn't at the gym or sleeping in the car, I'd hang out at Barnes & Noble. I was never good at school but, sitting by myself in the corner at the bookstore, I could actually learn. The reason I started hitting up Barnes & Noble was to read *Ring* magazine and anything else about MMA, wrestling, or jujitsu that I could get my hands on. I didn't have the money to buy them at the time, but sitting there was free. I soaked up all that knowledge without spending any money, studying up on what dudes were doing for strength and conditioning or fight preparation. I finally realized, shit, basically any question I had, I could read a book and learn more. I remember seeing this photo of Muhammad Ali reading a book called *Psychological Warfare*. I thought, *Man, if Ali is doing it, that means I gotta be doing it.* I started reading psychology books to try to get an advantage. I'd get a book on a topic that I was interested in and I could read it for two or three hours, leave it, and then come back and do it again another day. When I got bored of the fighting books and magazines, I started reading history books on conquerors and books on how people made money or about what happened in Cuba. I was getting the education at Barnes & Noble that I didn't get in high school. I was totally antisocial during this period of my life. I was either training at one of the gyms, by myself, or with my mom. And that was it.

I was always the youngest guy in the room with guys who were pushing thirty and had dozens of fights under their belt. But they took me under their wing. They told me I had raw talent and time on my side and that I just had to stick with it. I was still too young to fight professionally, but I started finding opportunities for unsanctioned street fights. It didn't matter if it was with gloves or bare-knuckle. We'd go wherever we could throw down: the back of a school, some LA Fitness gym, a local playground, or an empty pool. Anywhere. My friends were my promoters and matchmakers, finding someone from the neighborhood for me to fight. We'd put money on the line and go at it. I never lost one of those street fights, because the rules were different. We just fought until somebody quit, and I never did. I made a few hundred bucks from each of those bouts, just enough to get by. Whenever I won, me and my friends would go to McDonald's and go crazy at the Dollar Menu.

I remember one day me and some friends were posted up, eating cheeseburgers in the parking lot, when some fool kept driving by, staring me down. He did one lap, then another. As he drove past us he kept showing me his gold grill. Back then I didn't tolerate that shit. "Why are you staring at me, bro?" I shouted. "You're not a dog and neither am I, so why are you fucking showing me your teeth?" He stopped the car and started talking shit, so I started fighting him through the window of the car. He drove off. We stayed in the parking lot like idiots, eating cheeseburgers and yelling at all the girls who pulled up to the drive-thru. "Hey!" They bought us even more cheeseburgers. Eventually, the guy rolled back around with his crew. They parked the car and got out, and we dropped the cheeseburgers and started walking toward them. One of his buddies recognized me from the gym and told his buddy not to fight. They got in the car and left.

I couldn't wait to fight for real. I always knew I was meant for this prizefighter shit

KIMBO'S BACKYARD BRAWLS

I was a wide-eyed sixteen-year-old kid when I first saw Kimbo Slice. Back in the day, YouTube was like the Wild, Wild West with people posting slugfests. When I saw the video of Kimbo stomping into the backyard, all intimidating with his big beard and built like a brick shithouse, I was captivated by his presence and raw power. It was ba-fucking-nanas. Kimbo and his crew were taking over Miami.

Kimbo and his manager, Icey Mike Imber, were pioneers when it came to street fighting. They recognized the appetite for backyard brawls, and fans couldn't look away from Kimbo's devastating power. Icey Mike was a marketing genius: he knew how to create buzz. Mike would set up matches in people's backyards or on quiet streets and film them. Mike would upload the fight to YouTube, and it would pull in tens of millions of views.

Back when Kimbo was blowing up in popularity, every young fighter like me wanted to meet the legend. After there had been rumblings for weeks that Kimbo and his team were hunting prizefighters, I was laying on the mat one day when I heard he was coming to Freestyle Fighting Academy. *Shit, Kimbo is really gonna come to our gym?* The thought excited me, but the first two times Kimbo was supposed to visit, he didn't show up. But sure enough, as I was getting ready to train that day, a badass Lincoln limousine rolled up. When the door swung open, smoke poured out like a volcano. There he was, Kimbo Slice, walking into the gym with Icey Mike and their bro, the rapper Black Rob.

Kimbo's presence was intimidating. People were hesitant at first, not knowing if they could approach him for a picture, but it turned out Kimbo was cool as hell, man. Once one guy asked, suddenly everyone was lined up for pictures. Kimbo and his crew started visiting the gym regularly, and it wasn't long before they noticed me sparring in MMA. I remember him saying, "Bro, you're good. You're quick as fuck!" I made it clear to Icey Mike that I was down to fight in one of Kimbo's backyard shows. Not long after that, Icey Mike asked if I was serious about fighting. "Deadass," I told him. Back then, those street fights were illegal. Cops would shut them down and hand out tickets for being a public nuisance. The whole process of arranging the fights was hush-hush. Kimbo's team would be cagey with details and never reveal the location until the last moment. I'd get a call to confirm my interest—"Hey, you still wanna fight?"—with a promise they'd call me back with the location of the fight in three weeks. But three, four, five weeks went by with no call. I was in the McDonald's drive-thru when someone from Kimbo's team finally called, asking what I was up to. "You still wanna do this fight or what?" they asked. I didn't have shit to do, so I ate the burger, picked up a couple of friends for backup, and drove to the laundromat location Kimbo's people sent me. Kimbo pulled up in a black Cadillac Escalade, opened the door, and again, just like the first time I saw him, volcanic smoke flowed out. He took off his big chain, put it around Icey Mike's neck, and made a grand announcement. "Let's go!" he shouted. Kimbo fought first, no warm-up, nothing, and knocked his opponent out with a few punches.

I had no idea who my opponent would be when I arrived at the laundromat, and I didn't much care. It was just another fight. Then walked in Kimbo's protégé Reynaldo "Rey" Fuentes. Rey was a bouncer in Miami, and he had a reputation for being a tough guy. At the time, in the bare-knuckle-fight world of Miami, when it came to *Let's just fucking throw down*, Rey was the best guy. He was undefeated and dusted everyone he faced. Rey won the first three fights Icey Mike set up, so Icey Mike booked him two fights in one day. Rey was forty pounds heavier and close to a decade older, pretty much a grown-ass man compared to me. As I said, that didn't intimidate me. I was a skinny, 165-pound kid in baggy jean shorts, with high-top black Nikes and a ponytail. I've never lacked confidence. In my mind I've always thought, *I'm going to find a way to beat you up.* I thought I was better.

Rey was on a hot streak when I pulled my white T-shirt off and stepped into the makeshift ring behind the laundromat. He followed Kimbo and fought somebody else, knocking him out in a few seconds with one punch. Everybody went crazy. "Ponytail is about to get swiped out of the earth," I remember them saying, referring to the nickname Kimbo had given me. "Rey is gonna kill him. Are you stupid? Rey is gonna kill him." Almost all the side bets were on Rey.

Kimbo was like the fucking king of that world. There could be 1,000 people and if Kimbo said, *Shut the fuck up*, it would go silent. And when Kimbo said, *Party time*, it was go time. When they cleared the other fighter out, I walked through the gate and stepped right up.

I was giving Rey knees when he knocked me to the cement. Looking back, I should have stayed down longer but I got right back up like an idiot. That shit hurt. Every time I went at Rey, I made it a point to hurt him. So when he'd throw those big shots, I'd counter and hit him. I slowly broke him down with my shots to the body, one after another after another. Rey started circling, eating punches, and landing a few of his own. After four and a half minutes of jabs and punches, he was spent. He threw in the towel. "We got someone new on the block now!" someone said as they poured water on my head.

I didn't notice until afterward because of the adrenaline, but I split my elbow to the bone and cut open my chin when Rey dropped me early in the fight. I was broke and I didn't want to spend the thousand bucks they just gave me at the hospital. I knew they had to treat you at the public hospital, so I went to Jackson Health with a fake name and address. "What happened?" they asked. "I fell off my bike and hit my chin and busted my elbow," I said. They stitched my ass up and I took off. When I finally got back to my phone, I had missed several calls from the owner of the gym. Kimbo and his team wanted to take us out for a steak dinner. I had never experienced anything like it before. We walked into this fancy Brazilian restaurant in Fort Lauderdale, Chima Steakhouse, and Kimbo ordered a mountain of food. The doctor at the hospital had given me painkillers and I could barely eat despite the massive spread.

Absolutely nothing happened after the first fight. I didn't even know if it had been videotaped. Nothing showed up on YouTube for months. I had done scraps for money since I was sixteen, so, for me, it was just another fight. But Kimbo and Icey Mike knew we had magic in that backyard. A few months later they set up a rematch between me and Rey in the grass behind some Miami apartments. Rey trained for the rematch. He was more prepared, but so was I. In just a few months I was up to 177 pounds of lean muscle. The second fight was another battle. Rey dropped me again with a shot and, Lord have mercy, my head was spinning. When I got back up on my feet, this grown man was barreling toward me, ready to finish. I dug deep and turned the tables, forcing Rey to tap out for a second straight loss.

I didn't think much about the fights until a gym buddy called one day asking if I had seen myself on YouTube. Kimbo's team had finally dropped them and they were racking up hundreds of thousands of views. It was my first notoriety. *This is good*, I thought. I saw the online hype as my chance to get noticed by big promotions. I never cared for street fighting; it was just a means to an end until I could go pro for real.

I may have been the new kid on the block on the streets of Miami, but the world was about to know the name Jorge Masvidal.

CHAPTER 5

" GAMEBRED "

I was sitting in another 8:30 a.m. rah-rah meeting at that telemarketing job in Sarasota when I decided I wanted my first tattoo. The boss wanted to pump up our spirits with his motivational nonsense, but I couldn't give two shits about it.

That job was the same old story, day in and day out. I'd stumble into the office, my head pounding from too little sleep. We started cold-calling at 9 a.m., but they insisted we had to drag our sorry asses in by 8:30. God, I hated those meetings. It was like watching a rerun of the world's most boring TV show, with the boss trying to convince us that this job was our ticket to success. I settled into my cubicle, where I recited that same script over and over again for hours on end. Sitting there with my headset on was like being trapped in a never-ending loop. And then, to make matters worse, there was the second shift, 7 p.m. to 11 p.m. I'd finish one soul-sucking shift just to start another. There was no time left for training, no time for the gym. It was a fucking depressing time. I felt like a caged animal. I hated the office life, but it was a means to an end, and it was the only kind of work I could hold down. I was going back and forth between that and training, hustling to scrape together as much cash as I could to support Mama Dukes and me until I could turn pro.

This ain't ever gonna be my life, I told myself. I was neck-deep in the rat race now, because I had to pay the bills, but I was just chasing money to get by. I knew then that the typical office job sure as hell wasn't for me. Even if I could make bank sitting in an office, I knew that lifestyle wasn't what I wanted. I saw other guys raking in $60,000 or $70,000 a year and thought, *That's a shitload of money*. But I didn't envy them. I didn't like the way they looked or how they carried themselves. Nothing about them appealed to me. It wasn't their fault. They were sitting on their asses all day to make a living.

I was trying to be an athlete, but I could hardly train during those months, just squeezing in runs here and there, sometimes a session on the bag if I was lucky. It was one of the longest stretches I went without training. I had been training two or three times a day before that gig. But I had to hustle just to survive until the next paycheck and then scramble to get some training in until the money ran out again. It was a shitty cycle. I had trouble getting up early after staying up late from those crap hours. I'd get home late and couldn't fall asleep, so I'd eat and watch TV until 1 a.m. Nothing in my life was ever balanced. I'd gotten in such damn good shape and then would let myself go for months. Then I had to start over again. I was pissed off. I'd wasted all that time and effort. After all those office hours, I could feel myself getting soft, losing my edge. One morning it hit me: *I'm becoming less of an animal. I'm getting domesticated in this office*. I had to follow rules and all that bullshit. That's when I decided to get my first tattoo. I needed a statement, something bold. It was going to be my message to the world, a mark of my commitment to the game, a promise to myself that I'd never be chained to a desk again.

From the moment I first saw one, I was a big fan of American pit bull terriers. I loved those dogs. On one of my trips to Barnes & Noble,

I found some books and started reading up on them. The history of the American pit bull fascinated me. When they first came over from England in the 1800s, English bulldogs didn't look like they do today; they were these taller, leaner, stocky dogs—badass brick powerhouses. It didn't take long for people to notice the bulldogs were good at fighting, so they started pitting them against each other. Back then they had something called bullbaiting. They'd chain a bull in a ring and let loose ten pit bulls, thirty-five or forty-five pounds each. The steer would whip its head and send them flying. The goal was to latch onto the bull's nose, get him shaking, then pin him so he couldn't move. They'd let the dogs scrap and see which ones were the gamers. Some dogs wouldn't go; some dogs would. The dogs that weren't scared of the bull were game. Afterward, they'd breed the winners, the ones who were game, who weren't scared of nothing, who could take the pain and fatigue and keep going. That's how they bred them, the toughest of the tough, the ones that wouldn't back down from a fight. It was a savage world. The puppies that came from that litter were prized. Eventually, other dogs, like rat terriers, got thrown into the mix. They started breeding the most game, battle-hardened dogs together, generation after generation. That's how the American pit bull terrier was born—the highest evolution of pit bull. Real gamers, ready to take on anything.

I used to rant about this shit to my friend John, someone who had seen me scrap since I was fourteen. "Look at these dogs, man," I'd tell him, showing him a video. Every decent fighter has a nickname, and when it came time for me to pick one, I asked John what he thought.

"That's a no-brainer," John said. "Gamebred."

I never hesitated. It didn't just sound cool; it had a lot of meaning behind it. "Game" means the ability to fight through pain and fatigue. It's not about your skill level or if you're good, bad, or a world champion; it's about your willpower. "Bred" means being bred for this life, a life of fighting that I felt I was born to live.

Now I had a nickname. It was the last piece of the puzzle and I was ready to leave office work behind. I decided I needed to make it permanent. My friends had been getting tatted since they were twelve. I heard about this tattoo artist through a couple of older friends who had some ink done and their pieces were decent. My tattoo was simple: just "Gamebred" in big letters. So me and a few friends headed over to a friend of a friend's house to get inked up. It wasn't exactly a licensed shop. But I watched the guy wipe down his equipment with cotton swabs and put a new needle in the gun. *What could go wrong?* I thought. It wasn't the brightest idea, but I was a young knucklehead, too ignorant to be nervous.

"Where do you want it?" he asked.

"Right here," I said, pointing to the left side of my neck.

This was before neck tats were a thing, so it was a big fucking statement. It was my way of saying: *I'm married to the game.*

The guy got partway through writing "Gamebred" on my neck when he got to the second half with red ink. Apparently, I'm allergic to the red shit because my neck immediately flared up. We didn't even finish in one session, my neck swelled up so fast. It hurt like hell, but I came back later to finish the job. More pain, more swelling, but fuck it. No pain, no gain, right? My whole life, when I feel pain, I give it back even harder. Run until the hurt stops you. You get punched, you punch back. This time I had to just sit there and take it as the needle pierced my neck. After all that, I finally had it: "Gamebred" inked right on my neck for the whole world to see.

It was a stamp that I'd never be domesticated, would never join the "normal" world. I would rather die fighting, living in my car, chasing the dream, than be in a fucking office. I couldn't get a job back when I didn't have the neck tattoo, and I sure as shit was never getting hired with it on my neck now. That was fine with me, because I was going to make my money fighting. Every stab of the needle etched my new identity.

From that moment on, I was Jorge "Gamebred" Masvidal.

DREAMING IN THE 305

The UFC came to Miami for the first time after I turned eighteen. Back then we didn't have internet or smartphones, so I didn't even know about the event until three weeks before. Let me tell you, I couldn't stop thinking about it. I wanted to be there so bad. Lucky for me, John, who had helped me choose my nickname months earlier, bought tickets to UFC 42 and didn't tell me. That's the kind of dude he was. The tickets were probably $100. He wasn't rich or anything, just another kid working in Miami. He had a job and he was more focused on getting money. Me, I just worked to sustain my fighting lifestyle.

It was a sick-ass card that night, a stacked card from top to bottom. And the arena was empty. That's Miami. On any random night, there could be some big-shot performer in town, and half the city would be really into it. The other half, well, they're just there for the party, the drinking, to be seen. Miami people are last-minute for everything. They walk up to the box office and buy tickets on the spot. UFC wasn't part of the culture back then, not like it is now. This was 2003, a different era. I remember our original seats were in the rafters, but it was so empty, we moved to the lower level. We got as close as we could without getting busted by the ticket checkers, from the nosebleeds to the high-rises. Ended up with some pretty good seats. I still remember that night like it was yesterday. I'm not good with names or faces, but when it came to fighting, I was a nerd. For this stuff, I saw you once and if you were a good fighter, I remembered your name, where you were from, your style, your moves, everything. These were my rock stars and this was my livelihood.

At first, I watched with awe. *Wow, my first UFC fight. There's so-and-so just hanging out in the crowd. That's crazy!* I was a fucking nerd just going nuts. Pete Spratt submitted Robbie Lawler. Rich Franklin knocked out Evan Tanner. And Matt Hughes beat Sean Sherk in the welterweight title fight. Seeing those guys that night cemented it: *Yeah, I could do this. I was meant to do this. Every cell in my body was created for this.*

From that moment on, there was no turning back. I knew I wasn't as good as these guys—yet. I had a long journey ahead of me, a life that would be defined by blood, sweat, and sacrifice. But that was the theme of my life. I sucked at this, so I worked to get better at it. I didn't have this, so I went and got it. I had to take control of my destiny. The world was going to know about Jorge "Gamebred" Masvidal.

Miami had made me, but the Octagon was where I belonged.

BEGINNING WITH A BANG

The day I turned eighteen, I was ready to enter the cage. My pro debut couldn't come fast enough. I just needed someone to give me a fight. Not long after I attended UFC 42, my chance came. Someone at the gym got word from a promoter about a fighter who had dropped out of an event. They needed someone to step in at 150 pounds. *Boom!*

"You wanna fight?" they asked me.

I didn't hesitate. I was hungry, and I thought I was invincible. It was time to see if I had what it took to defeat seasoned vets. My coaches didn't want me to take the fight. This other guy wasn't great, but he wasn't some schmuck who had never fought. He had a lot of professional experience. A few months earlier, he'd submitted a dude in under ninety seconds with an arm bar.

"You sure? This guy's experienced," my coach said. "I don't think it's a good first fight."

"I'll be fine," I told him.

It was risky to go take an early *L* in my career. I didn't care. I figured if I hit this guy once, it was over. They sent me some video of the guy. He had a bad record: 6 wins and 7 losses. I watched two or three fights.

"I'll fight him," I said. "Let's go."

I was eighteen, so I could sign and drive. That's exactly what I did.

I dropped ten pounds and on May 24, 2003, exactly one month after I watched my first UFC fight in Miami with John, I drove half an hour north up I-95 from Miami to Fort Lauderdale, Florida, to fight Brandon Bledsoe at Absolute Fighting Championship 3. I was fighting on the undercard of a small Florida show—nothing major, but I knew it was the real deal when I walked into the arena and Bruce Buffer was announcing. "Weighing 150 pounds, representing Freestyle Fighting Academy, fighting out of Miami, Florida, please welcome . . ." I got a thrill hearing Buffer announce my name for the first time: "Jorge Masvidal!" I stood in the tunnel, listening to Buffer drag out those syllables, soaking it all in. That was it: my dreams becoming reality. I wasn't nervous at all. The only people there were some longtime friends and my coaches. Mama Dukes skipped my early fights and Papa Dukes was still locked up. They wouldn't have been there long anyway.

The fight barely lasted four minutes. I caught the guy with a few crisp jabs—left, right, left, right—and sent him to the mat. First-round knockout, just as I'd predicted. I made a grand that night, $500 to show, $500 to win. It wasn't much, but it was enough to keep the dream going until the next fight. That first thousand-dollar check was a game-changer. I finally had real prize money, not just pocket change from gigs. But the thing was just a piece of paper until I got it to the bank. My bank account was pretty much empty. I was broke leading up to that fight, having spent everything on training just to get there.

The promoter put me up in the Radisson after, standard for those fights because the guy owned the hotel. My friends all went out partying on Las Olas Boulevard to celebrate. But I wasn't even twenty-one. I went back to my room, took a hot bath, and walked down to the Waffle House to eat. It was a modest celebration. I won but knew I had a long way to go. Most guys who get a first-round KO against a veteran let it go to their head. Not me. I got taken down once. At that moment, that's what I took away from the fight. That showed me there were holes in my game. I knew what I was good at but focused more on my weaknesses. I needed a lot more work to get to where I wanted to go. My hands were quick, but the gas tank still needed work. Grappling tired me out fast too. I went back to the gym, back to the grind. There were no shortcuts, no secret path—just hard work.

I always looked at it this way: I had to stay good at what I was naturally good at, but I had to work twice as hard to bring up my weaknesses. Take Mike Tyson, for example. In his prime, he was untouchable, undefeated, killing everybody. But put him up against a decent wrestler, and unless he landed a killer shot, four out of five times he'd get taken down. His striking wouldn't matter once he got taken down. I knew that would be the same for me. You can't do nothing on your back. I had speed and power, but if any good grappler put me on my back, it was over. All this fucking speed and power goes to shit. I had to fill in those holes.

I always went after what I was bad at. If I kept getting caught in a move, I'd practice that position until it became second nature. Fundamentals were my foundation. I spent most of my early career working on defensive tactics: how to stuff takedowns, how to escape bad positions. From fourteen to twenty, my skills developed significantly. I didn't want to wrestle. I wanted to stay on my feet, learn how to defend, get back up if I got taken down, and get back to throwing punches.

THE PERFECT START

After that first win, I signed with Absolute Fighting Championship (AFC). They had some big names from the UFC and top title challengers. It was the perfect proving ground to test myself against skilled fighters and get noticed.

That first year I fought five times in less than twelve months and won them all, but it meant living at the gym nonstop. There was no consistent fighting schedule; it was almost always a last-minute phone call from the promoter. "Hey, you wanna fight in three weeks?" I didn't have time to get ready, so I had to stay ready at all times. I wasn't going to get in shape in three weeks; I had to be in shape already. It was a different lifestyle living in the gym.

My paychecks gradually increased with each fight. The promoter bumped it up by $100 each time. I fought nine times with the AFC in Fort Lauderdale over the years and worked my way up to a final pay-check of $1,200 to show and $1,200 to win. Selling tickets sweetened the deal. If I could sell tickets, the promoter would throw some money my way. I was a ticket-selling machine even back then. At that time I had a lot of friends—friends, acquaintances, and hangers-on—and the promoter relied on me to help fill the seats. But selling those tickets and collecting the money was a fucking headache and a half. It was like I was back out there hustling again. Still, I was a good salesman. I took any fight I could and pocketed a few hundred dollars extra from ticket sales, but it still wasn't enough to sustain a life.

I always had a side hustle to make some extra cash. I could write a book on how many different gigs I had. I told you about some of them. Catering, petting zoos, moving companies, demolition work, and lawn care. On weekends I helped my uncle remove carpeting and nail in baseboards. During my first professional year, my boy John got me a job at a law firm he was working at. They needed stenographers to transcribe court proceedings. This was back when they used CDs to record everything in court, and I'd take summary notes of it all. *The judge offers blah, blah, blah . . . five years mandatory probation, blah, blah, blah . . .* You know, all the CliffsNotes. John got me this job and everybody working there could type 60 words a minute. I couldn't type more than maybe 10 words a minute. But it paid the bills.

Other professional MMA circuits had scouts who traveled from show to show. If they saw an up-and-comer take down an ex-UFC fighter or a guy with a good record, they'd take notice. I was beating good, experienced guys in those early fights but no scouts noticed me. I wasn't on the radar for the major promotions yet, even though I was undefeated. I couldn't get the recognition I deserved because I didn't have a manager or a team behind me. I wasn't getting called to the next-level shows.

The odds were low to get into the UFC. Even lower to stay in the UFC. Back then if you lost one fight, they'd show you the door; if you lost two fights, you were history. I was so headstrong, I didn't give a flying fuck about the odds. I knew I could beat these UFC guys if I had the proper training camp. They weren't tougher than me. They weren't better athletes than me in the sport of fighting. Maybe they could play basketball or football better, but in the sport of fighting? Not a chance.

I just knew that if I could get to the big show, everything would be all right. Knowing how far I'd already come from fighting in the streets, nothing could convince me otherwise. The odds were just numbers. "Just trust me, Mama," I'd tell Mama Dukes. "Everything's gonna be all right. I'm gonna keep working and keep giving you a little bit of money here, a little bit there, and then if I get to this big show, I'll kick all those guys' asses. Everything's gonna be okay." That was the plan.

CHAPTER 6

TURNING LOSSES INTO LESSONS

I fought five fights in less than twelve months during the first year of my professional career, a perfect 5-0. I felt unstoppable. Knockouts, unanimous decisions—it was the perfect start. But then, like a Muhammad Ali punch to the face, everything came to a screeching halt.

Life has a funny way of teaching you lessons you never thought you needed to learn. It was during this time that I learned one of the most valuable lessons of my life: nothing is ever as good or as bad as it seems. When I reached the end of that first year with a 5-0 record, my confidence was soaring high. I felt invincible. I was sure I was destined for the UFC in no time. But then reality hit me like a sucker punch to the gut. All of a sudden, I couldn't get a fight to save my life. It was like someone had pulled the rug out from under me and I found myself on the mat, struggling to get up.

For nearly a full year, from May 2004 to April 2005, I didn't fight. It's a twisted game, this fight business. I was good, I was tough, and I had skills, but I was still a nobody in the MMA world. So the ranked guys avoided me. People demanded more money to fight me and promoters flinched and flaked. A lot of guys who were just as good as me—with records like 5-0, 6-0, 7-0, or even 10-0—didn't want to fight either. Why would they? They didn't want to risk their record against some up-and-coming fighter like me for shit pay. I wasn't a big name yet. If I'd had more name recognition, maybe I could have gotten the fights I wanted. And, man, I tried. I would have taken anything. The bigger names didn't want to face me unless there was a scout in the audience. They'd look at me and think, *This kid is young, he has some speed, he has some power, he's been training forever. It's a tough fight for no money. Why do that?* I can't say I blame them, but damn if it wasn't frustrating sitting on the sidelines. It was a harsh reality check that knocked me down a peg or two. But that's the thing about life, about this fight game: it's a roller-coaster ride of highs and lows. One moment you're on top of the world, your hand raised in the air victorious, and the next you're lying on the mat, beaten down and a fucking bloody mess. The key, I realized, was not letting the lows define you. And let me tell you, there were lows.

With no fights booked, I slipped back into doing dumb shit to make some cash and get by. For a few months I was just chasing money and being a young, hotheaded kid. I'd let loose and party, but that was the least of it. I got injured in the gym one day and let myself fall out of training for a while. A whole month went by without me going to the gym. My coaches came by the house one day: "Bro, what's going on?" they asked. I was dealing with financial troubles and I was trying to make ends meet any way I could. I needed money to provide, so I tapped old connections from the streets, did things I ain't proud of. At one point growing up, Mama Dukes's house caught fire and they cut a hole in the roof to put it out. Can you believe that? Insurance didn't want to pay for it. They thought my mom had had something to do with it. It took, like, four fucking years to get that roof fixed, and for the first six months my mom couldn't even live there because the house was condemned. After that, when I couldn't find a fight, I ended up moving back in with Mama Dukes for a year in that burnt-down, half-destroyed place. The walls were black. There was a giant hole in the roof—a hellhole. Those were dark fucking times. We had no money, and I was working hard to take care of my mom. I'd get home from whatever bullshit I was doing and the lights were off. That wasn't a surprise most of the time because they'd probably been off for two weeks because me and Mama Dukes couldn't pay the power bill. All the food in the fridge was fucking rotten without electricity. The house was like an oven in the Miami heat. Fucking A. Bad times. Our only option was to hustle.

Training for fights that kept falling through was disheartening. Busting my ass for months, with no job and no regular income, training hard, prepping for a fight, and then *bam!* Canceled. It happened more times than I can count. Promoters calling me up promising fights that never materialized. The other guy pulled out? The promoter ghosted? *Fuck!* I was left hung out to dry with no payday in sight. Some other promoter would call saying he had a fight for me in two months. *Yeah, right, they're probably bullshitting me.* I was stuck in this cycle, doing half-assed training and picking up half-assed jobs to keep a roof over my head. I did a little bit of both to make enough to get by, because if someone pulled a fight again, I'd be evicted from my fucking car at that point.

Hustling was all around us in Miami. I had chosen to break out of that life, but when you're starving and desperate, old temptations creep back in. Fighting was my dream, but it wasn't putting food on the table—not when I was an unknown fighter watching his career stall out. I started doing some not-so-legal hustling and shit to survive. The Miami hustle, you know? If things fell off a truck and my friends happened to work at the right places loading those trucks, well, I'd have five PlayStations to flip real quick to make some extra cash.

For anybody from Miami coming up back then, we didn't see no doctors or lawyers; we grew up seeing drug smugglers and dealers. That's what was around us. You had to choose, because that life was in your face 24/7. I found myself at a crossroads that could easily derail my dreams if I chose wrong. It would have been easy to give in to the quick money and fast life. But deep down I knew I needed to break out of it for good.

BLESSINGS FROM ABOVE

I know, sure as hell, I'm not perfect and probably don't deserve half of the blessings that I've received in my life. But one thing is for damn sure: I believe God has been looking out for me for a long time. I still don't know why.

I was five years old, living with my grandparents in Peru, when I encountered something that changed my life forever and made me realize there was something else out there, something beyond what we can see. It was a moment I've never felt before or since, like it came from a different dimension or a different planet. I had just arrived in Peru not long before, and I was knocked out, fast asleep on the bed. If you ever go to South America, you'll see a lot of houses have these big wooden walls, almost like garage doors, that act as room dividers. They go up to the ceiling and are ten feet wide. My grandparents had one of those massive walls to separate the bathroom from their bedroom. While I was sleeping on the bed, my grandma was on the other side redecorating the bathroom. *Thump!* It was like something shoved me right off the mattress. Before I realized what was happening, I was on the floor. When I opened my eyes, that massive wooden wall came crashing down onto the bed right where I had been sleeping. It hit the bed so hard that it broke one of the legs. My aunt rushed into the room screaming. "What did you do?" I didn't know what the hell she was talking about. I was in shock and could hardly say a word. "I didn't do anything," I managed. "I was sleeping!" Eventually, the whole house was in the room, asking me what had happened. I tried to talk, but I couldn't get a word in. I couldn't explain it; it was the weirdest thing I've ever felt in my life. I knew then that there was something supernatural, something I couldn't comprehend.

For weeks and months I couldn't stop thinking about it. That was the first time I encountered God's presence. I had so many questions racing through my head. *If I hadn't been pushed off that bed, what would've happened to me?* I didn't know what to believe or who to ask. I never mentioned those thoughts to my family. I was a little kid and figured they'd think I was crazy. My grandma was a devout Catholic. She said the rosary—fifty Hail Marys, the whole deal—every day. We were on our knees daily saying the Our Father. My grandparents lived by that.

At some point not long after that, my grandma gave me a Bible. I was intrigued by that Bible because so many inexplicable things had already happened in my life. I thought that book was going to explain everything to me. My grandma would take me to church and I learned to pray. A lot of times I just prayed by myself in my room. In the beginning I prayed a lot to see my mom. I would have given anything to see Mama Dukes again. My grandma would tell me to say twenty Hail Marys and then I could say what was really in my heart. The more I read that Bible, the more I questioned my grandma about it. I asked her one day, "In the Bible, it says you're only supposed to pray to God and Jesus, so why are we praying to his mom?" She looked at me like I was stupid. "That's the Virgin Mary!" she yelled. Grandma only laid her hands on me a couple of times, and both times were about religion, me being a smart-ass. I was so religious back then, my family in Peru all thought I'd become a priest. From the time that door incident happened until I was nine years old, my aunts and my grandparents were all convinced. I was busy reading that Bible, praying my heart out, stuck in this weird place, wondering, *What the hell happened?* I didn't have friends, no mom, no dad; I was just by myself in a foreign country. So, yeah, they thought I was going to join the Catholic Church. Ironic, isn't it?

As I grew older, I didn't actively practice any religion by reading the Bible or going to church, but that encounter with God as a kid never left me. I remained convinced that some higher power watched over me, even if I didn't fully understand it. That belief was tested during my year away from fighting. With no fights to keep me on the path toward my ultimate dream, I was desperate and tempted by old connections from the streets. I came close to making poor choices that could have ruined my dreams. But divine intervention set me straight once again.

Until that point in my life, I was no saint. My dad had always warned me to never sell drugs no matter what or I'd end up locked up like him. One of the guys I knew growing up stayed in that world, and during that year when I couldn't find a fight, our paths crossed again. One day he hit me up with an offer, telling me about a big drug shipment we could rob. He was getting all his information from one of his friends who had just gotten out of jail. He laid out the whole plan, said they needed one more guy. "Not a chance," I told him. "I ain't doing it, bro." I knew better than to get involved in shit like that no matter how tempting the promise of quick cash might be. I went home and as soon as I walked in the door, Mama Dukes was having a horrible episode. We were running low on money and she was taking out her frustration on me, throwing plates and calling me a fucking bum. The rent was due any day now. I had enough for that month's rent, but for the next couple of months I was going to have to stop training again and pick up gigs. It was going to fucking suck. I called the guy back. "What's up with this fucking thing?" I asked. He started talking, "This is the plan," he said as I zoned out. "Blah, blah, blah."

The guy picked me up and we scoped the place out, planning to hit it in a few days. As we drove, something in the back of my mind kept eating at me: *Don't do this*, a voice was telling me. All I could think about was what Papa Dukes had warned me about for years. I had visited that federal prison enough to know I didn't want to be locked up in one of those fucking cages. I was uneasy for the next couple of days, but I agreed to tag along. When the day came, the doubts crept back in. I called the guy and told him I wasn't sure if I was going to do it, that I'd hit him back after I took a nap to clear my head. I went home and passed out on the bed.

The next thing I knew, these dudes were picking me up at my house, suited up in masks and dark clothes. Adrenaline pumped through my veins as we pulled up to the house. I smashed the window with my elbow, reached through, and unlocked the door. These other dudes had weapons drawn, ready to grab everything. But the place was empty. "You idiots are too late," some guy inside said. "They already took everything. You fucked up." We ransacked the place anyway, searching every drawer and closet for any scraps we could find. After a few minutes I got a bad feeling we needed to get out of there fast. I grabbed a set of car keys and jumped into the truck parked outside. The other guys followed with the measly shit we managed to scrounge up.

I floored it out of there, whipping through the neighborhood streets. Out of nowhere I spotted a police car, lights off. As I looked through the mirror, I saw the car make a U-turn behind us. I stepped on the gas, weaving left and right, trying to lose him. I looked back; I didn't see him. One of the guys knew this area well, so he told me to stop and let him out. We slowed to fifteen miles per hour and he rolled out and disappeared into the night. I kept driving, but soon the streets started crawling with cop cars blocking every turn. Everywhere I looked, there was a cop car a few blocks down the street. Helicopters circled above, scanning the ground with spotlights. It was a full-on manhunt closing in on us. There was no other option now: we ditched the truck and ran to hide in someone's backyard. I was buried under leaves and branches, heartbeat going crazy, as the helicopter spotlight traced along the pitch-black ground. I was fucking freaking out. *This is it.* I closed my eyes and started praying harder than ever before. I told God, "If you get me out of this, I swear I'll never commit another crime as long as I live!" As I was praying, the spotlight slowly swept over me, then started drifting away.

Guess what happened? I snapped awake covered in sweat. *Holy shit, it was just a dream!* I had told the guy I was going to take a nap and had fallen asleep for five hours. I looked at my phone; I had two missed calls from the guy. While I was asleep, they went on the robbery without me. One of the guys got busted later for stealing a car on that job. But me—I took it as the ultimate sign. It was the craziest dream ever. It was like I had been there, like God had transported me to show the consequences if I went down that path. I never committed another crime after that night. Sure, I threw fists to defend myself if someone stepped on me—even in the Bible God says it's okay to defend yourself—but no more shady business.

I never wanted to live that life my dad warned me against. Maybe all those years visiting him behind bars were God's way of setting me straight. My old man was the guardian angel on my shoulder, keeping me from following his footsteps. That dream coincided with everything. I decided I wasn't going down that dark hole. I made a U-turn right then and there. God gives us signs; we just have to look for them. I'm convinced that dream and some higher power saved my life. I'm living proof that, with faith, even the lost can find their way. You simply have to believe and leave the rest to powers greater than yourself. It's not the destination that matters most; it's staying true to the journey.

LESSON LEARNED: BE IN CONTROL

I built my whole career on last-minute fights when some other fighter would bail on a card. The promoters would hit me up: "Hey, Jorge, want to grab this spot in three weeks?" Hell yeah. I didn't have a big pedigree or amateur background, so it wasn't like promoters were trying to build a card around me. I took all the fights nobody else wanted. I just loved scrapping and was convinced I could take out any of the so-called contenders. I didn't give a fuck if I was going to his hometown, his crowd.

That's how I got my first bout after that shitty year of no fights and almost pissing away my career on South Beach. Same old story. Some guy dropped from a card near Atlanta ten days out. The opponent was a Georgia boy with a big local following. It was like if you would have fought me in Miami or Fort Lauderdale. But I needed that money and he had a good name. I knew one of us would likely catch the eye of the UFC after the showdown. There were a lot of pluses for me, so I fucking did it. I lost a shit ton of weight and went to a Podunk town just outside Atlanta to fight this 4-0 guy named Raphael Assunção. He'd never fought outside Atlanta in his professional MMA career and now I was in his backyard. In my mind, I felt like I whupped him in rounds two and three. But wouldn't you know it; the judges robbed my ass and gave the decision to the hometown hero. Straight-up highway robbery.

Five-and-one. That was my first loss, but I definitely, sure as hell, didn't lose the fight. Just what I thought were the corrupt judges in Georgia. I crossed paths with them later in my career and they said, "Man, I gave it to the other guy, but you won that night." I looked at them and told them, "Yeah, I get it, you motherfucker." That's how my career rolled; I went to their backyards, dominated them, and still got shafted by the judges. That's how it is when you're fighting as an outsider. It was a theme, a part of my brand since I was a kid. The road was my home, and as long as they paid me, I'd go there and beat the shit out of anyone. Japan, England, Russia, Costa Rica, Philippines—I fought in all these places, and each time it was just *Let's go. I'm here to do this.* I loved it.

One lesson hit home hard after Georgia: Stop taking short-notice fights and avoid fighting in the opponent's hometown. Well, I guess I didn't learn it, because I kept doing that throughout my whole career. The need was too great. Those opportunities, even with just a few weeks' notice, could mean the difference between making rent or not. I had a mark on my record, but I didn't let that first loss slow me down none. After that Georgia fight, promoters started realizing I was a tough out. Managers began hearing about me because on ten days' notice I had been expected to get steamrolled by Assunção, who was seen as an up-and-coming Brazilian jujitsu wizard. Yet I almost snapped his arm with an armbar. After that, the fights kept coming, one after another.

As I was getting the Assunção fight signed on short notice, I was already in talks with the AFC, the promotion I'd been competing for, about another short-notice fight. I told them straight up, "Yeah, I'm gonna do your fight no matter what. I got this fight in Georgia. I'm gonna go break that guy's face and I'm gonna show up to your show and break that guy's face too. You guys okay with that?" They didn't seem to mind. That Assunção fight went down on a Thursday night in Atlanta. Just nine days later, on a Saturday night, I stepped into the ring again, prepared to face a future UFC Hall of Famer, Joe Lauzon. I was still lumped up and bruised, with a black eye, my shin sore from all the kicks, and with a swollen hand, but nothing ice couldn't fix. I was ready. I weighed in and took care of business. All the anger I had from getting robbed in the fight the week before I took out against Lauzon. I decided after that "loss" to Assunção I wasn't going to leave my fate in the judges' hands. I was never letting another fight go to a decision if I could keep it in my hands. In fighting, that's not always easy. Sometimes the other guy doesn't want to fight; he wants to play it safe, score points, and run. Trying to finish him or getting into situations where you could hurt each other doesn't happen as often as you'd like.

Lauzon was a whole different beast from Assunção. Assunção was calculated, more methodical in finishing, but Lauzon was overzealous, eager to get a finish. He'd put himself in bad spots and go for it everywhere. He had one of the highest finishing rates and the most submissions in the UFC by the end of his career. I took advantage and landed punches. I didn't leave any doubt against Lauzon. The judges had no say. I sent him out on a stretcher, oxygen mask and all. It was brutal, worse than a TKO. You have to watch that fight. It's on YouTube. Fuck, that's one of the worst beatings I ever handed out.

I felt like I was undefeated until I fought Paul Rodriguez. I 100 percent believe that. After I knocked out Lauzon at AFC 12, the promoters immediately put me on the card for AFC 13 three months later. Just like that, I was signed to fight Rodriguez. He was an ex-UFC guy, experienced and talented, with a nasty overhand and some solid chokes. I'd seen him fight before and I knew he was well-rounded. Facing him early in my career was risky. He had just come off the UFC and was looking to get signed again; they just needed him to grab a win or two. He was on the brink of a comeback. He came in overweight by four pounds. He promised, "No matter what happens, I'll give you a rematch." Rematch? "Whatever happens, give me that rematch," I said. "I'm gonna knock your ass out, bro." I got cocky and sloppy, and I got caught. Early in the round, he took me down, but I managed to sweep and get on top, unleashing a barrage of punches. We went from one side of the ring to the other, and I went for a big flying knee and got cracked midair. The timing wasn't bad, but as I launched it Rodriguez caught me with a right hand because my technique was shit. It dazed the hell out of me. He took my back and put me in a rear-naked choke. I fought the choke and defended well, but my body gave out, and I passed out cold. My first real loss. He had caught me clean, choked me out unconscious, no denying it. That's a fight.

Throughout my career, losses taught me more than wins. That loss to Rodriguez in particular was pivotal. I asked my coaches what went wrong, dissected every mistake. That's how it goes. You learn more from catching an *L* than racking up another *W*. After I came to I was pissed—at myself more than anything. *Fuck!* I was doing well. I didn't need to rush it. I went for the finish with sloppy technique. It stung, but I learned more from that than any win up to then. It was that loss where I learned the flying knee. I went straight back to the gym and practiced that flying knee over and over and over. I studied other fighters who threw it flawlessly, determined not to let it happen again. For some time after Rodriguez choked me out, I would go from my workout straight to flying-knee training. I kept having this image of me throwing the knee, taking the hit, being dropped, and getting choked out. I couldn't tell you how many times I practiced that knee because of the anger and the frustration of losing to this guy who I thought I was ten times better than.

The thing about defeat—in anything in life—is that it either breaks you or makes you. At your lowest point, there are two paths: lower or higher. I learned real quick that all the depression and self-pity, all the fucking bullshit, would pass no matter how deep it felt at the time. So I had a choice: sit on my couch and stare at the TV, or go after my goals relentlessly. Losses lit a fire under my ass. They made me push harder, train longer, and become a better fighter. If I was running three miles a day before, I was going to run five now. After a loss, I'd focus on improving whatever weakness got exposed. I knew my strength was striking but my grappling needed work. So I drilled defensive wrestling relentlessly, knowing that's where I could be exploited. Of course, I sharpened my stand-up too. But shoring your weaknesses makes the real difference. If you stay hungry after a setback and fill those holes in your game, you always come back stronger. This guy Rodriguez shouldn't have been holding my jockstrap, but he caught me because I made a technical mistake. In my mind, my career was set back by three, four, maybe even five fights because of that mistake, that loss. Who knew how many I'd have to win to get the UFC's attention?

I went on an 8-0 rampage over three years after that loss. It took three years undefeated between then and 2008 before I started attracting more attention. Life humbles everyone eventually. How you handle adversity defines you. There ain't no shame in taking an *L* when it fuels you like that. You either let it break you or you get back to the grind hungrier than ever. I learned that lesson real quick. I chose to let my failures turn me into something stronger. It was those early setbacks that prepared me and gave me the skills and mindset to survive and thrive on the biggest stage. That flying knee became one of my best weapons. I knocked fools dead with it thanks to losing that way. Funny how it goes.

CHAPTER 7

CHAMPION MINDSET

*The fight is won or lost far away from the witnesses—behind
the lines, in the gym, and out there on the road, long before I
dance under those lights.*

—Muhammad Ali

That Ali quote was plastered on the wall of the boxing gym I stepped
foot in every day growing up. As a kid, I saw the flashy highlights on
TV: Ali dropping fools with his lightning hands, Foreman crushing
suckers, Frazier slugging it out until the final bell. The appeal and glory
of the big fight night. I wanted that spotlight bad. But that quote was a
reminder that being a fighter was more than the glamor I saw on pay-
per-view. It stared at me every time I laced up my shoes and put on my
gloves, reminding me of the truth that the fight wasn't won when you
were basking in the glory of the spotlight but far away from the ring or
the Octagon, deep in the trenches of the gym. To make it in fighting
took more than just talent. It took endless hours of blood, sweat, and
tears when no one was watching.

I'd spend hours at the gym watching lifelong fighters train, soaking up every bit of knowledge those guys would share. I couldn't tell you the square root of shit, but when it came to fighting, I was an encyclopedia of knowledge ever since I had been a young kid. I could recall those locker room conversations with older fighters like they were etched in my brain. They shared their experiences and little gems, the kind you can't find in textbooks, about what it took to succeed in this brutal sport. Growing up around those fighters and idolizing their culture, I stuck with it. I read books about the major champion boxers because, back then, MMA wasn't the behemoth it is today. Those books held the secrets of their workout routines, their lifestyles, their work ethics, and their mindsets. I'd read them cover to cover, dissecting every page for nuggets of wisdom.

The real sacrifice happens far from the cage when no one sees you vomiting through another gut-check workout or refusing to pig out at 2 a.m. when you wake up hungry. It's easy to look like a killer under the bright lights. It's the unglamorous grind in the shadows that separates the elite from the rest. You're jumping rope, you're running your miles, you're doing your sit-ups, you're doing your push-ups, you're doing your crunches, you're throwing your punches and getting punched in the face, you're getting kicked, you're getting kneed in the ribs. You're doing that over and over and over and nobody's watching you doing all that work. And when the bright light does come on, it just doesn't happen. You have to go out there and get it.

Guys like Ali stood out not just for their talent and charisma but the conviction behind it. Sitting out his prime for his beliefs, unafraid to sacrifice everything for what he felt was right. That was true greatness to me. It inspired me to keep grinding in obscurity until my time came to dance under those lights. But the fight would be won or lost in those quiet moments in training when I was pushing my mind and body to the brink, not sitting on the couch, pigging out, or taking shortcuts. The road to being the best is often a lonely one. One more round of sparring when your hands are busted up, one more mile when your lungs are screaming. Embrace the long grind, stay true to yourself, and then, when the spotlight hits, just let it all hang out. Fortune favors the hard workers, not the entitled. That was the biggest lesson I took from fighters like Ali coming up. And it served me well once my time came to shine.

THE GRIND OF FIGHT WEEK

The lead-up to fight week was a grueling ritual, a relentless battle with the scale and my mind. When I was competing at 155 pounds, I'd walk around at a solid 180 pounds. And so, when fight week arrived, the countdown to weigh-in day began. When a fight was on the horizon, it was time to make that excruciating cut down to 155, the lightweight division I fought at early on in my career.

If I had a fight scheduled on a Saturday night, I'd arrive on the Sunday a full week before. It was an entire day of traveling, but I usually picked Sundays because I wasn't doing shit on Sundays anyway, so why not spend it traveling? I would diet down to around 174 pounds by the time I got on the plane, but at that weight I was still only 5 percent body fat. The real challenge was still ahead. I'd arrive in whatever city we were fighting in on Sunday already knowing I had 19 pounds of water weight to cut to make the 155-pound mark.

Like clockwork, when I arrived, I'd go right into my schedule.

SUNDAY

I would land in the fight city on Sunday. It was the calm before the storm. The first order of business was to check my weight, a reminder of the brutal week ahead. If the number on the scale read 174 pounds,

I had a lot of work to do but I was on track. Sometimes I'd do a bit of pad work on that travel day, just a light ten or fifteen minutes, to shake off any jitters from the flight and get back in the groove. Time to get acclimated and mentally prepared for the grind ahead.

MONDAY

Monday was when the real grind began. I'd wake up early and go for an hour or more jog or run on the treadmill at a fast pace. Sometimes I wore a hoodie and sweats and others I wore a sauna suit to get a good sweat in and drain as much water weight as possible. I could drop five pounds that first workout, bringing me down to 169 pounds. Hydration was crucial, so I'd drink water throughout the day, even as I lost weight. After the run, it was more cardio, light pads, jumping rope, three five-minute runs—just constant movement. By the end of that workout, I might have lost another two pounds, bringing the total for the day to seven pounds.

Post-workout, I'd refuel with a small meal: salad, egg whites, and a shit ton of water. It might seem counterproductive. You just lost that water weight; why are you putting it back? Staying hydrated was essential. You don't want to be dehydrated before the fight. I had to test my body's limits to see how much weight I could safely cut. There's a science to it. After lunch, I'd get a little bit of rest and check my weight. I might be back up to 172 pounds, so I'd squeeze in another thirty to ninety minutes of training, whether it was pads, jumping rope, or wrestling. Another weigh-in. One hundred and sixty-nine pounds? Not bad. I'd drink a bunch of water and go to sleep.

TUESDAY

Tuesday usually started with me weighing around 170 pounds. It was almost a repeat of Monday. Wake up early, hit the treadmill in all my sweat gear, and run for an hour. More sweat, more weight lost. Without much food in the previous forty-eight hours, I'd start feeling a bit lightheaded and drained at this point. I'd gather my bearings, sit down for a bit, and stretch out. Then it was back to pads and jumping rope, constant moving and sweating, just slowly chipping away at the weight. If I finished the day at 165 pounds, I was in striking range of making weight.

WEDNESDAY

Wednesday was when I started to take things a bit slower. I didn't want to exhaust myself before the big weight cut on Thursday. I'd already been cutting calories and all I had was salad, fruits and veggies, and tons of water. I was feeling sluggish. When you're cutting weight like that, you've got no life in you. I didn't want to look at my shadow, didn't want to hear from or talk to nobody. I just wanted to do my job and get the fuck out. It might have appeared like I was being antisocial, but during fight week I was incredibly focused and selfish about my time and energy. I couldn't afford distractions. My mind was fixated on what I needed to do in the fight; everything else faded into the background. I was constantly visualizing, running scenarios through my head. They always said you had to have an A, B, and C plan in fighting because there were so many variables. You could easily get lost in your thoughts, thinking about how to react if your opponent did this or that. It was an endless mental exercise, preparing myself for every possible situation that could arise in the Octagon.

THURSDAY

Thursday was the day when the real weight cut began. It usually started anywhere between 4 p.m. to 6 p.m. No more food. I was even done drinking water—maybe a little sip if I felt like it. But that was it. I might start the day around 165 in the morning and needed to shed seven to eight more pounds, and that was on my light days. Sometimes

I'd wake up Thursday at 168 pounds. My goal was to go from 165 pounds in the morning to between 158 and 160 pounds by bedtime. My head would be spinning by then. If I sat down and my coach called, I'd get up and feel dizzy, like the entire world was off its axis, hanging on to the wall just to stand. The next morning it would all come down to the final weigh-in.

FRIDAY

On Friday morning it was time to wake up and cut the remainder of the weight, usually three or four pounds. The goal was to step on the scale and see 156 pounds or less. If it wasn't a title fight, you got that one-pound allowance. I'd step on the scale, head spinning, completely depleted. It was a weeklong struggle, but I never missed weight. That entire week up to fight night was a fight in itself right there. That was the lifestyle I lived for a long time. And after that hell of a week, shit, the fight seemed easy.

X X X

After I made the cut, I'd start replenishing immediately: guzzling water, IVs in both arms. Back then IVs were legal, so I'd take two and rehydrate within hours, going from 156 pounds to 180 pounds overnight. I felt like a new man by the time I stepped into the cage Saturday night. Eventually the United States Anti-Doping Agency outlawed IVs because they thought there was a chance they could be used to mask steroids. When they did that, it was the straw that broke the camel's back. I immediately went up to the 170-pound welterweight division. I couldn't keep cutting weight like I had for so much of my career. It was still a grind, but at 170 pounds, fight week became a bit more relaxed. I could focus on technique and strategy instead of solely cutting weight and feeling exhausted.

It took years off my life, cutting weight like that during every camp. But it's what you have to do to compete at the highest level. The public just saw me on fight night, not the hell I walked through all week. That's the price you pay to make it in this sport. There ain't no easy roads to the top. You either embrace the grind or get left in the dust. There are so few fighters who make it to the UFC. I knew guys just as talented, or more, who didn't have the work ethic or luck to get there. Shit, I got lucky. A kid from the streets who found his way out. So many guys I grew up with ended up in jail, or worse, without the opportunities I had. I thank God for my dad guiding me as a voice of reason growing up, showing me the dangers of that life before it consumed me.

But it wasn't just luck. Plenty of guys had talent but didn't put the work in. The sacrifice, the cost, what I've paid to be a champion . . . Too many people only see the highlights. They only see the periods when I'm on top and they think that that's what life is. It's far more defined by the periods they can't see. They don't see the long days in the gym, the 4 a.m. runs, the brutal weight cuts, the injuries and setbacks.

The real test is when nobody is watching. When it'd be easy to sleep in, cheap out on your diet, skip that last rep. But you embrace the grind and push through. Luck is just opportunity meeting preparation. You create your luck through relentless work. It's easy to think champions are just born different. But the greats are made through sacrifice that's unobserved. You want to be the best? Then work while your competition rests. Stay hungry while they get complacent. Be the first one in and the last one out day after day. Keep believing through the setbacks and criticism. That's how you make it to the show. Luck favors the prepared and hungry—in fighting *and* life.

FIVE KEYS TO SUCCESS

1. FAITH IN A HIGHER POWER

I grew up very poor and very hungry, skipping a lot of meals and watching everyone around me have more. But I also knew there was a higher power watching over me. I had faith in God and belief that if I worked hard, my day would come. Whether you place your faith in God, the universe, or any other force, having a belief that there is something greater than yourself can be empowering. It's not about who you pray to or what beliefs you hold but rather the understanding that there is a purpose to life and you're part of a larger plan. That belief became my anchor during tough times. It didn't matter who or what I prayed to as I grew older; I didn't constantly read the Bible or go to church after I left Peru. What mattered was the unwavering faith that I could change my circumstances. No matter your background or circumstances, faith can be a powerful driving force. Trust in yourself, work diligently, and believe that every challenge you face is an opportunity to rise and improve.

2. UNBREAKABLE SELF-BELIEF

In the fighting world, the highs and lows come fast. One minute your coach reminds you to keep your left up and you avoid disaster; the next you get dropped hard in the gym sparring. That's when belief is tested most. I'd get my ass whupped and get humbled. Then I would look for a way to fix that problem, come back harder, and see the results. I had to evolve constantly, understanding that even losses were lessons. Whether it was waking up at dawn to run four miles or pushing through hardships, I kept my unshakable belief in myself. I knew that at some point my day was going to come if I refused to give up. The champions I looked up to in boxing and MMA all had that same unshakable belief in themselves too. It didn't matter who they fought: they believed they would win. I realized that, along with hard work, I needed that belief in myself to push through the difficult moments and keep evolving. To believe in yourself, you have to believe at all times—when you're winning and losing, at your best and worst. Embrace challenges as opportunities for growth and keep evolving no matter the setbacks. Never give up on your journey to success.

3. MAKING SACRIFICES

I didn't have shit growing up, so sacrifice wasn't new to me. Getting up early to run miles on an empty stomach sucked. But I wanted a better life for me and Mama Dukes. Electricity going out, bouncing around from place to place—I knew deep down that I didn't want to live that life. What was the formula for getting out of there? Sacrifice. Since I didn't have much, I sacrificed comfort for my goals. Waking up early to get another session took priority over chasing girls or going to a club. You have to align your actions with your dreams. I was born in 1984 and faced plenty of distractions. There are a million more today. Your mind is racing everywhere. In a world filled with diversions and easy choices everywhere, I learned if you want to succeed, you have to have a dedicated, singular focus. You have to pick one passion, dive deep into it, and know all the ins and outs, A through Z. Find your passion and put the work in day after day. Even on days you don't feel like it, force yourself to put in that extra hour. There are no shortcuts to greatness. Embrace the grind. You have to love the process to get to the destination. Nothing great is achieved without hours of practice and preparation behind it. Natural talent only goes so far. You've got to put in the time and outwork the competition. Prioritize your goals over immediate pleasures, and recognize that distractions can sidetrack you from your path. There is no success without some sacrifice.

4. AVOIDING THE EASY PATH

Often in life there's a hard path and an easy path. Most take the easy one. Something in me was drawn to the difficult road. Fighting, to me, was a way of life, a means of controlling the chaos. There were days when I was tired as hell, beat up, and my leg throbbed from taking a brutal kick during Tuesday night's sparring session. On the drive back home, I couldn't even bend my leg. But I knew that I had to wake up at 6:30 a.m. and run those grueling four miles. It was going to be painful. Every step was going to fucking hurt. But I understood that completing that run was going to get me that much closer to breaking my opponent's face in the upcoming fight. So I didn't give a fuck about the pain. I was going to put that aside and get it done. The easy path is just to do what everybody else does; the harder path is to create your own way. For many people, the easy path is to go get a job and work for the Man. The harder path is going out and creating your own environment, your own dynamic. The path to success isn't always easy, but it's often the most rewarding. Don't be afraid to blaze your trail, even if it means confronting difficulties, pushing through pain, and choosing the less-traveled road.

5. FINDING YOUR PEOPLE

I didn't like my environment as a kid. The gym was my safe space growing up. No matter what chaos or negativity surrounded my life, I could go to the gym and work on my skills, and my day would get better. I fell in love with the grind. When I started joining gyms, I learned that you become like the people you surround yourself with. If you surround yourself with negative people who aren't going anywhere, you'll likely end up in the same place. But if you surround yourself with people who share your passion and drive, people who lift you higher, you'll achieve more than you ever imagined. That's why I chose the gym and not the Miami streets. I started surrounding myself with people who worked as hard as me, who motivated me to keep grinding. We fed off each other's energy and desire to improve. Iron sharpens iron: when you have a strong team pushing each other, special things happen. That's what happened at American Top Team. Building the right team isn't easy. You have to find people who share your values and vision— people who complement your strengths and offset your weaknesses, who align with the vision you want to create. You need people who pick you up at your lows and challenge you at your highs. I succeeded because I built relationships with people like my striking coach Paulino, who brought out the best in me, people who shared my relentless drive to put in the work day after day. If you want to go far, surround yourself with people who make you better and propel you higher.

CHAPTER 8

TURNING POINTS

One thing about fighting is it can humble you quick if you get too cocky. I learned that the hard way when I arrived at the gym one day in 2007 and my coaches told me I'd be sparring a guy named Paulino in practice.

I'd heard stories about the dude's sick tae kwon do back in Cuba, but that had been a long-ass time ago. He had been living in Bolivia, teaching tennis lessons or some shit, and was just getting back into MMA. My coach claimed he was the best guy he'd ever trained with. "Bro," I told him, "there ain't no way." I was already beating the crap out of 10-0, 15-0 pros in the gym daily. In walked this scrawny fucking dude. It didn't look like he had a muscle on his body. I was twenty-two, so I was considerably faster than everybody that I ever worked out with. This wasn't a time to spar with me. This guy wasn't even ranked, hadn't been training MMA for years. I figured I'd take it easy on the old man. Big mistake. I learned so fucking much that day. Never, ever, ever, ever—as much as I thought I knew about fighting—judge a book by its cover.

We got in the ring and after we touched gloves this guy proceeded to beat the shit out of me for four straight rounds. He didn't just beat me—he gave me a fucking whupping. He fucked me up every which way. He out-pointed me, outdid me, out-slicked me, out-quicked me, outthought me. I couldn't land a thing, while he tagged me at will. It was a master class.

After the beating Paulino gave me, I sat by the bags stunned, exhausted, and feeling empty. I was in peak condition, coming off a recent fight and training for the next one. But none of that mattered. This dude styled all over me with minimal effort. He hadn't necessarily hit me hard to the head; it was just how effortlessly he beat me and I couldn't time his move, couldn't do anything to him. *What the fuck? There's no way he just beat me up like that*, I sat there thinking. *What the fuck is wrong with me?* It was a serious blow to my ego; it made me question everything I thought I knew. I got beat so badly, I didn't know what direction I was going to take in fighting.

Paulino walked over to where I was sitting; he saw by my body language and the beating I had taken. "Bro, you got a lot of talent," he said to me in Spanish. "You're as good as they say." I was shocked he was taking a liking to me. I figured he saw me as straight trash. He wasn't patronizing me. He actually wanted to help. "We just need to focus your talent and get it right," he said. He told me he could show me some things, change this and alter that. My skills were incomplete but I had so many gifts, it was only a matter of time before I'd catch up with other fighters. "Whatever you say, bro," I told him. "I'll jump through a fucking concrete wall." I wasn't about to turn down guidance from the guy who just schooled me.

We started working together once a week. Then twice. Before long he was essentially my full-time striking coach. My other coach was never around, off with other fighters. One week he was with me in Miami and the next week he was gone in a different state, in a different country, in God knows where. I was starting to get more fights, bigger fights, bigger names, more money. And this guy wasn't around. But Paulino was there consistently, three, four, even five times a week, no questions asked.

Me and Paulino were grinding daily, and eventually my other striking coach got jealous, wanted to set times for him versus Paulino. "Motherfucker," I told him, "you're never here, bro." Around then I was still training regularly at Freestyle Fighting Academy as a big part of my gym rotation. It was a small up-and-coming team of pro fighters and we were ready for the next phase. I'd been with them since they opened when I was just fifteen. The team was close: they had dinner together every Sunday. So when they asked me to sign a contract to officially join their team, I didn't think twice. I trusted these guys. I didn't read the contract much—nothing like that. *They wouldn't do me wrong*, I thought. So I fucking signed the thing.

Next thing I knew, I was getting ready to go to my second gym one day when they stopped me and said Freestyle wanted me to do all my striking sessions in-house with their coaches from now on. It was a new phase as the gym grew. I was confused.

"Do you want me to tell my coach to come here?" I said to the guys. "Because he has his own gym."

"No, no," they told me. "We're only going to use our striking coaches for the striking."

I thought they were deadass joking with me. But, no, they were serious. "We already got all the head coaches here for the striking," they said. "We feel like you should work with them." That's when they brought up that I had signed the contract. I felt fucked. *These fucking pieces of shit. They got me. Bro, what?*

One thing about me: Never give me an ultimatum. And never mess with my loyalty to Paulino. Paulino was the guy I would never get rid of, no matter what. The guy was my fucking everything. He took me off the streets and saw my potential. He told me, "If you put all the bullshit, all the street life, to the side and focus on this, you're gonna go so far, and I'm gonna be right there with you." We had a handshake deal to split my earnings. All he wanted was 5 percent of whatever I earned. If I didn't make $1, then Paulino didn't want $1. But if I made $100 million I'd give him 5 percent. It was the fairest deal I'd ever heard in my life. We still have that deal to this day.

I went straight ruthless street fighter on the Freestyle guys, flipped the switch on them so fast. "All right, you got me on the paperwork," I said. "I thought you guys were good people. But, nah, that paperwork isn't gonna count." I told them they'd better shred that contract if they knew what was good for their gym. They'd known me since I was fifteen on the streets, so they knew I could bring a tidal wave of fucking problems. They backed off pretty quick and voided the contract but said I was banned from training there. Fine by me after the stunt they'd pulled. I told Paulino, "Bro, I'm gonna rock with you forever. I don't care about no gyms, no coaching, no nobody. You're my coach for life, man." He became my striking coach for my entire career. Whatever he told me to do, I fucking did it. A lot of the sharpening of my technique, fundamentals, and strategy over the years was thanks to him. Loyalty is everything to me. I felt that FFA betrayed our history. Paulino proved himself time and again.

I trained in every gym across Miami as a teenager. From east to west, north to south, Miami was mine. My striking was on point and there were good jujitsu programs around, but Miami was missing top-level wrestling training and a true MMA program. After the whole Freestyle Fight Academy debacle, I found a gym in Arizona and was ready to move me and Paulino both out west. Paulino was ready to go. "If that's where we gotta go for six weeks to get you ready, we'll go there," he told me.

But then Ricardo Libório caught wind of me. He had cofounded the renowned Brazilian Top Team gym and was then head coach at

American Top Team in Miami. I had fought some guys from American Top Team, so they knew me. Through a connection, Libório was asked about me and was apparently impressed. "He's a fucking beast," Libório said. "If he had the right type of training, that kid could go far." The news got back to me that American Top Team wanted me to try out and Libório was the guy who set it all up. I told Paulino we could stay put in Florida after all. The missing piece had fallen into place right in my city.

Libório got me in the door, and American Top Team provided the complete MMA training I needed to round out my game. My striking was already elite thanks to Paulino. Now I finally had access to top-tier wrestling and Brazilian jujitsu to take me to the next level. It was perfect timing and a perfect fit. Ricardo saw my potential and helped open the door. Paulino molded me into a creative striker. And American Top Team gave me the full arsenal to become a complete mixed martial artist. My career finally had all the elements in place.

DREAMS COME TRUE

I'll never forget the day we got the call from Papa Dukes. I was just finishing up a training session with Paulino, our first fight camp together, drenched in sweat and catching my breath, when I saw the missed call from Texas. I picked up the phone and listened to the voicemail. "I'm on the way to Florida," Papa Dukes said. "I've just been released." We all scrambled. We didn't even know what flight he was on; we just went to Miami International Airport and waited there all fucking day to see if he walked out of the terminal.

I was in shock. After nearly nineteen years locked up, Pops was finally coming home. I hadn't seen him outside of a prison visitation room since I was four years old. He had already finished his twenty-year sentence months earlier, but since he was a Cuban refugee, he had nowhere to go. If you're not a U.S. citizen, you normally get deported, but since the U.S. didn't have a treaty with Cuba, he couldn't be sent back. So they sent him to Texas and tossed him in an immigration detention center for an indefinite period. It was the ghetto-est shit you've ever heard of. Then, after nine months on top of his sentence, they just released him. We posted up at the airport and waited for hours, searching for Papa Dukes in every face that walked through the terminal exit. When he finally walked out of the gate, it was surreal. Papa Dukes standing there in front of me, a free man. I barely recognized him out of his prison jumpsuit. I hugged him harder than I ever had. No guards screaming, "No contact!" Just me and him, together again after almost two decades apart.

I was on the verge of a career breakthrough when my dad was released from prison in April 2007. Papa Dukes had never seen me fight in person but he'd been following my career from prison. I used to train and spar with some correctional officers and SWAT guys, showing them moves for cash on the side. It just so happened that one of them worked at my dad's prison and ended up being a fan of my early MMA fights. Small world. He was one of the higher-ranking correctional officers at the prison and knew about my career from the local scene. One day he had asked my old man, "Is that your boy, Masvidal?" When Papa Dukes said yes, the guard told him, "I've been watching your son work out for two years. He's an animal." Long story short, I would buy Cuban food and the guard would come to my house, take it to the prison with his lunch, and give it to my dad. He never got to see me compete live in those early years, but later on this guard would let him get on the computer to watch some of my early fights on YouTube.

A few months after Papa Dukes was released, I was scheduled for the biggest fight of my career to that point: Yves Edwards on a Bodog

Fight card. It's like the universe knew my dad was coming home. I was in the middle of a five-fight contract with Bodog, and the fight with Edwards kept getting pushed back and pushed back. This was going to be the first fight my dad was ever going to see, and on top of that it was going to be against the highest-ranked opponent I had ever fought. Edwards around that time was No. 2 or No. 3 in the whole fucking world. I was, like, No. 115. This was my shot to put everyone on notice. This was *the* moment in my life.

X X X

At the beginning of my career, I grinded my ass off, doing everything I could to get a UFC contract. I tried desperately to get on one of the first seasons of the *Ultimate Fighter* show in 2005. They had this sweet deal where they'd put all these fighters together in a house in Las Vegas and follow them around while they trained and fought each other. Every up-and-coming fighter wanted a spot on the show to fight for a prized six-figure contract with the UFC.

The winner essentially received a three-year deal for three fights a year with guaranteed money the first year. The first year each fight was $12,000 to show, another $12,000 if you won: $24,000 per fight. Second year was $16,000 and $16,000: $32,000 per fight. Third year was $22,000 and $22,000: $44,000 per fight. Guaranteed $150,000 with a chance to double it? Sign my ass up! I thought I had a real shot but found out they had an age requirement: you had to be twenty-one years old so the fighters could booze it up in the *Ultimate Fighter* house. Those first seasons I was twenty years old—shit out of luck. That was the closest I got to signing with the UFC early in my career. I was certain I was going to end up in the UFC Octagon, but there was going to be no easy path or quick shortcut there.

Instead of competing for that six-figure UFC contract, I was back to my AFC deal, which was a long way from that dream. When I won my eighth and final fight with AFC in 2006, I think the purse was $1,200 to show and $1,200 to win. I walked out with a unanimous decision and $2,400. That win, combined with an 8-2 start to my MMA career, caught the eyes of Bodog Fight. Bodog signed me to a five-fight contract that gave me a chance to change the trajectory of my life. Let's say I was making five grand a fight before; for this fight I was making $20,000 flat—win or lose. I started my Bodog contract with two wins in 2006, setting me up for the biggest fight of my career to that point: a matchup with a dangerous MMA vet.

Yves Edwards was huge. He had a highlight reel out there to terrorize the fighting community. I say "terrorize" because he was knocking people unconscious. He had several nicknames—"the Dentist" being one—because his trademark move was a knee to the face that he used to knock guys' fucking teeth out. He had literally shattered several dude's upper palates with that move. It gave me chills watching it. I told myself, *I'm not going to let that happen to me.* Yves was a left-hander who fought what he called Thugjitsu, which was a range of boxing, Thai boxing, wrestling, and Brazilian jujitsu. It was a bad matchup for me in many ways, and honestly, of all the guys I had fought, he was the one who gave me some butterflies. He was a nightmare at 155 pounds. I had seen what he had done to his opponents. I was just a twenty-two-year-old kid with a 10-2 record compared to the thirty-year-old Edwards, who was 31-12-1. It was the biggest challenge I had faced in my career.

I studied his tape relentlessly and knew I couldn't afford any mistakes against a finisher like him. I trained like a madman leading up to that fight, running myself into the ground because I didn't want to get my face rearranged like I'd see happen to other guys—especially with Papa Dukes in the crowd.

Because of the federal probation system's restrictions, my dad couldn't fly, so he drove eighteen fucking hours up I-95 from Miami to Trenton, New Jersey, to watch me fight. My best friend, John, my old friend who helped coin my nickname, drove up too. My people didn't get the greatest tickets back then. I didn't have a name or anything, so I was just the guy who was supposed to get his ass handed to him by a UFC all-star. My dad and John were somewhere in the stands at Sovereign Bank Arena, but I couldn't spot them.

Edwards came out hard, firing his patented kicks. He didn't hit me in the face, but he was throwing legs and body shots too. I stayed patient, just waiting and waiting, picking him apart, trying to get his timing down, and feeling him out. After the first round, my corner gave me some advice, and with about two minutes left in the second round, it happened. I found that sweet spot for a right kick and landed it square on Yves's jaw. I followed it up with a flurry of punches, and the referee stepped in to stop the fight: it was a second-round knockout. That is still one of the biggest moments of my career.

I injured my foot to secure the victory. During the first round, I kicked Yves in the leg, and my foot instantly started to swell. When I landed the final kick to his head, it ballooned to the size of a football. I didn't care. I'd just smoked this guy in front of my dad. We went to the hospital and sat there for a couple of hours before the doctor assured me my foot wasn't broken. Hell yeah! I had a massive hematoma but nothing I couldn't handle. I hopped around Jersey all night. We celebrated with pizza, hot dogs, whatever was open. We went from one place to another, pigging out and catching up on life.

I could see how proud Papa Dukes was. He couldn't believe what he had witnessed. He knew how good Yves was and he had been the one to tell me I could beat this guy. And when it happened, he was beaming with pride. I remember him telling me, "You see, everything that you've been doing, all that hard work, is finally paying off. You just have to stick to it."

That win changed everything—put me firmly on the map. And

getting to share it with my old man just months after his release took it to another level. My dreams were coming true.

A NEW PURPOSE

I never thought I'd have kids. Never, never, never, never, ever, ever. Not in a million years. It was the furthest thing from my mind. I was living the fighter's life, focusing on training, competing, and, well, being wild. But life has a funny way of throwing you curveballs when you least expect them.

I remember that moment like it was yesterday, clear as day. I had just gotten done fighting at the Playboy Mansion when my girlfriend called me. "Hey, oh my gosh, so what happened?" I told her the news. "I knocked the guy out." We celebrated a bit and she said, "I need to talk to you." I joked around. "Oh my gosh, you're talking to me," I replied. She got real serious. "No, I have to tell you in person when you get back." A few days later, when I got back from Beverly Hills, I was at the gym, paying coaches and training, when she said she was on her way over to talk. "Well, you got an hour and a half to get here," I told her. "I gotta leave. I can't be late to practice." An hour and a half went by and she was still stuck in traffic. "Yo, I gotta go," I told her. That's when she dropped the bomb: "I'll just tell you now over the phone. Fuck it," she said. "I wanted to tell you in person, but I'm pregnant, I'm keeping the baby, and I just want to know if you're gonna be part of the baby's life."

Fuck! I was shocked. The news was a bomb and a half. I stammered something about needing time to think and got off the phone, numb. My head was spinning. I went through the whole practice in a haze, not sure how to process this shock that life had just given me. I had some serious reflection to do.

My girlfriend had told me she couldn't have kids because of her family health history. Then *bam*, six weeks later she was pregnant. I was blindsided. I was a mess those first few weeks. If it were a movie, you'd see a montage of me crying alone in my car at night for a month straight after training. She said from the jump she was having this baby no matter what. I felt trapped at first. She already had a daughter, so it was like I was having two kids overnight. Talk about trial by fire. I was nowhere near ready to be a parent, let alone to two kids at once. I was the furthest thing from being a parent back then. I was a nomad, still couch surfing and making just enough to get by. It took me a month to accept it. I talked to Papa Dukes, talked to Mama Dukes, talked to everybody. Papa Dukes not being around when I was younger had caused me plenty of pain, not knowing where my dad was. I refused to put another generation through that if I could help it. This was the ultimate test: it was time to be a man.

When my daughter, Ava, was born on October 6, 2008, it was an out-of-body experience. I almost passed out seeing her covered in fluid, umbilical cord still attached. I couldn't even cut the cord, I was so shook. "Sir, are you okay?" one of the doctors asked as I turned pale. I couldn't even hold her. No fight ever paralyzed me like that.

The birth of my daughter changed everything. Suddenly fighting took on a different meaning. Fighting was no longer just a sport I loved; now it was a job and people were relying on me. There was real pressure to win and earn big purses. For months after Ava's birth, I struggled to fight with the same recklessness. I felt the weight of responsibility on my shoulders. I was fucking dead broke and all of a sudden I had to spend $400 a month on Pampers, $150 a month for formula, and more for day care bills. I had all these crazy expenses I'd never worried about before. It was an overnight switch to go from only worrying about myself to being completely responsible for four people. It took me a long time to get my mind back to 100 percent and approach fighting the same way I did before.

Years later, in 2015, I ended up having a son. Like Ava, he came unexpectedly. Me and my girlfriend were on and off for years, and after one of my fights in Orlando, I took the family on a cruise to Mexico. After a few too many drinks one night, I was worried about a slip-up. Six weeks later we found out she was pregnant again, and my little guy, Josiah, was born. I can't explain it, but our connection was immediate. Now I'm his best friend and he's mine.

As terrified and reluctant as I was initially, becoming a father was the greatest blessing in disguise. My daughter and son gave me a whole new source of strength. The sacrifices became more than worth it. I started to fight for them as much as myself.

CHAPTER 9

AMERICAN TOP TEAM

The first time I walked into American Top Team, my mind was blown. I was starstruck as I looked around the gym at all these guys I had seen fight on the big stage. There were three top-fifteen fighters in the world just hanging out. The No. 2 guy, the No. 5 guy, the No. 8 guy—no exaggeration, no bullshit. Gesias "JZ" Cavalcante, Marcus Aurélio Martins, and Din Thomas were all at the top of their game and they were getting ready to scrap in the same gym. I saw Brazilian ju-jitsu world champs just fucking chilling. I'd never seen so many ranked fighters in one place. If the average MMA gym had two or three big names, this gym already had twenty-five or thirty legit fighters, half of them Brazilians who had been fighting since they were five years old. I knew from that day that American Top Team was where I was supposed to be. It was the greatest fucking atmosphere. I was in heaven.

It just so happened that American Top Team was an hour's drive from my backyard. Around 2001, this rich dude named Dan Lambert met the guys who started Brazilian Top Team. Dan is a multi-multimillionaire who has enough money to not have to get out of bed in the morning. And yet the guy would get after it every day in the gym. He had a black belt in jujitsu that he *earned*. Dan loves fighting, so when he met these guys, he fell in love with MMA and had the idea to build his team using his business principles. So with Dan's backing and these guys from Brazilian Top Team, American Top Team was born in Coconut Creek, Florida, just outside Miami. Within ten years of its opening, Dan owned the best MMA gym by a mile.

Dan was the definition of "If he doesn't fuck with you, he doesn't fuck with you"; he either likes you or he doesn't. And if he's your brother, he's your brother and he's got your back. Everybody wanted to kill this guy because they thought he was a rich guy pretending to be a fighter. But Dan didn't back down. I always respected his character and admired that he didn't take shit.

American Top Team was full of alphas. I witnessed so many straight-up fights break out—not even training, just guys trying to kill each other. Coaches watched but didn't stop it. I remember thinking during the first fight I watched, *Oh, shit, this is what they do here. I gotta go for the fucking kill.* Iron sharpens iron, so if you can't hang, fucking leave. That was the attitude. Not everybody was cut out for it. I'd eat my lunch at practices and at night we'd have another session, so I'd sleep right on those mats. That gym was my temple.

In my first practice, I kicked ass. The coaches were impressed and saw major potential in me. But there were still a lot of holes in my game. My grappling was shit compared to the world champs there. At Freestyle Fighting Academy I was like a local legend. Once I joined American Top Team I realized how much I didn't know. They'd re-cruit the best Brazilian jujitsu champs from Brazil to train there. I went from training with wrestlers who didn't have any black belts and knew some jujitsu to world champion arm snappers who had grown up with jujitsu since they were five years old. During my first years at American Top Team, I was a fucking dork, tapping out nonstop. I was learning every day.

I could smoke everybody at my old gym but could never go 100 percent because they weren't built like that. I knew at American Top Team I had to give it my all just to hang and get to the finish line. That lit a fire under my ass because those guys were trying to kill each other. It wasn't like now, where they monitor hits; if you were getting ready for a fight, you just fucking fought hard. These guys would be going half-ass on each other, and then as the new guy they tried to kill me. It was a great time to learn and measure up against MMA's best.

American Top Team meant everything in taking my career to the next level toward the UFC. They had UFC fighters close to the top ten or fighting for belts. Numbers-wise—you could ask anybody—I was at the No. 1 gym in the world. I knew going into fights I'd trained with the best of the best. Sparring with those guys behind the scenes gave me confidence that I could go under the lights in the Octagon and murder people. I started going into fights knowing I'd been preparing with the best and there was no stopping me.

A NEW WORLD OF FIGHTING

Ever since I was a kid, I always wanted to fight in Japan. At 155 pounds, they had some of the best guys in the world in my weight class. The UFC was known for having bigger guys in the fighting world. In fact, they didn't even have the 155-pound division until UFC 26 in 2000. The top talent at lightweight was fighting in Japan. The best fighters from the Western world in that weight class were traveling to Japan, and it was on my bucket list to fight there one day. At the time, landing a fight in Japan was a significant milestone in my career. If you were competing there, you were doing well for yourself.

When I joined the gym, American Top Team already had some fighters in a big tournament in Japan. Two guys from my weight class were in it and there was this other tournament there from a promotion called Sengoku. The coaches were trying to decide if they should send a third guy over there. After the third fight of my Bodog contract, right after I beat Yves with Paulino by my side and Papa Dukes looking on, Bodog went out of business. I was back to struggling to land fights, back to the same shit, taking any fight I could get on a week's notice. It was a shitty time because I felt that I was worth something. I'd already beaten good guys and the UFC wasn't giving me the offers I wanted or thought I deserved. So I kept holding out and went to other shows to see what I could do. I was on a big eight-fight win streak from 2006 to 2008, beating a lot of dudes, including that knockout of Edwards, but I still wasn't a household name. Fighting in Japan was the chance to change that. The coaches ended up submitting my name and I was chosen. I was going to fight one of the biggest names at 155 pounds in Japan: a guy named Takanori Gomi, who was the lightweight champion of multiple big Japanese promotions. But then, just two weeks before the fight, they switched me to a completely different opponent with a different style. I still took the fight.

Flying to Japan was grueling: twenty-four fucking hours of travel. And I had the worst seats because I was a nobody. Promoters don't give a damn about you in the beginning. It was like a fucking movie. I was crammed in the back of the plane for fourteen hours. My first flight to Japan was the worst. I got a regular night of sleep and I had cut weight leading up to the fight, which meant I was running low on carbs, not eating much food, and drinking a lot of water. I played Tetris, meditated, did whatever I could to stay sane during those long flights. No matter how bad the situation was, I tried not to get bent out of shape. I didn't want to waste emotions. So I just sat there and made the fucking best of it.

I arrived a week early for that first fight. The long-ass flight to Narita Airport was followed by an hour's drive to the hotel. Fight night was another two hours each way by bus. Landing in Japan was like stepping into a whole new world. It was so clean, you could practically eat off the streets, and everyone was polite. I was amazed. But I didn't fucking speak Japanese, so they put translators with me all day. And I was dead broke, so I only had the per diem from the promotion to eat. Anything else I was saving for back home. We were hanging out with friends, making bets. Like, "Hey, if you snort some wasabi, I'll give you $100." The whole thing was like a movie. I was convinced I was eating the best fucking sushi in the world. Back home, I'd go to the cheapest sushi joints I could find. When you're broke, even the cheap sushi rolls feel like a luxury. So imagine me going to these sushi restaurants in Japan thinking every one was the greatest sushi ever. I was hanging with the Japanese translators one day, telling them how great one of the sushi restaurants was. "That is McDonald's sushi, the worst." Psh! I was arguing with them: "Are you fucking kidding me? Are you crazy? You don't know shit!" They always dished it back: "You don't know shit, you fucking dumb American!" They started telling me where to go for the *real* sushi. As I kept fighting in Japan— five times in total—I started going to the places they recommended. They were right; I was just a dumb American.

The Japanese crowds were knowledgeable about fighting. They'd been exposed to judo, grappling, kickboxing—all kinds of combat— since they were in school. And people in the audience were dead silent during the fights. It was the best place to hear my coaches, clear as day. When some big move happened—a beautiful throw or a nasty punch—the whole crowd, I'm not lying, would go, "Ahhh, oooh," in unison, like an orchestra. Exactly on point when something awesome happened. But otherwise no talking whatsoever. Imagine 20,000 silent fans invested in the fight. You could have a conversation or shout someone out and they'd hear you in that huge arena. It was totally silent, like a sign of respect.

In my first fight there, I came out to this insane atmosphere. The quiet tension before the storm. I could hear my coaches perfectly. I dropped this guy Rodrigo Damm in the first round. In the second round, he knocked me down with a right hand and as soon as my butt touched the mat the ref stepped in and stopped the fight. It was the weirdest thing ever. It wasn't a KO at all: I was fine. But my first trip to Japan was a loss by KO. It was a controversial, bullshit stoppage. The ref and the president of the promotion apologized afterward, but the loss was a loss. There's nothing worse than getting robbed like that. I was perfectly fine; I could have kept fighting. But sometimes that's the sport. It just means you have to fight harder and beat the fucking living brakes out of the other guy.

The two-hour bus ride back to the hotel after that loss was the most annoying bus ride on the fucking planet. Some of my coaches were bummed but one kept trying to flirt with the Japanese translators, telling me in Spanish to hype him up to these girls. "Tell her I'm a good kisser!" he said. I wasn't in the mood to hear anybody talk. I didn't want to be on that fucking bus. My mind was on every sequence of the fight, and this guy kept talking. "Bro, shut the fuck up," I told him. I told myself then that no matter what happened, I'd never do that loser bus ride again. I felt the loss was mainly the ref's fault but still on me too. I dropped the guy in the first round and let him put me on the mat in the second. I was definitely never trying to be on that two-hour bus ride with an *L* on the record again.

I fought four more times in Japan and never lost again, going 4–1 total there. I ended up fighting the Sengoku tournament champion later and knocked him out cold in round two. Satoru Kitaoka had only been KO'd twice in 43 fights before I punched him out. My promoter was hyped, so she took me to one of the premier Japanese steak joints, where they had exclusive meats you couldn't get in America. Stuff called Matsusaka beef that's several cuts above Wagyu. Back in 2009, an eight-ounce steak was $1,000. This stuff was unaffordable as hell. No way, no shit, no how could I have ever been purchasing things like that, but she hooked it up. After another big win, she took me to the iconic restaurant where they filmed *Kill Bill*, where we celebrated like royalty.

After three or four fights beating bigger names in Japan, I started getting more attention stateside. Japan was a pinnacle of fighting at the time, so the wins carried weight with U.S. promoters. I was making decent money in Japan, something like $30,000 per fight—win or lose. So when I came back to the States, I could negotiate better deals with promotions. "Hey, you want to sign me up?" I'd say. "This is what you gotta pay."

The UFC was lowballing me with offers. I was bummed because I saw the talent the UFC had and knew I could beat those guys. But they had to fucking pay me what I was worth. Maybe I was too money-hungry sometimes. Part of me regrets not going to UFC sooner and fucking going for it as a young fighter. But I've always been about getting paid. I loved fighting and was good at it, but I had to be compensated. I knew my value even back then. Since I was young, I believed you have to get paid for what you're good at. I was never willing to sell myself short. I always tried to get the best deal for myself. Who's offering the most? That was where I was going.

From 2005 to 2012, I moved around to any circuit where I could get a fight. From AFC to Bodog Fight and Bellator to Strikeforce, each stop gave me a wealth of knowledge and experience, seeing how the different shows operated. It struck me that every circuit seemed to be struggling to survive. I never knew when the next fight or paycheck would come.

MY TIME TO SHINE

A career-defining moment came in 2012 with Strikeforce. I'd racked up back-to-back unanimous decision wins at lightweight to get a shot at the Strikeforce title. Winner would get the belt and go on to fight the UFC champ. Loser? Who the hell knows?

But there's always a twist in my story, right? My buddy was fighting in the finals of a Bellator tournament in New Jersey. He asked me to corner him, sort of like being a coach for support. My coaches told me not to go corner him. "Hey, I know you want to corner this guy, but please don't go," they said. But I'm hardheaded and went anyway. I came back and got sick for ten days. And I had a sparring session where I couldn't move. Guess what? I threw a right hand and tore the fucking ligaments in my right hand clean in half. I hit my hand over the top of this guy's head and my fingers and wrist touched when the guy ducked. Ten days before the fight, my hand was fucked.

Even with my screwed-up hand, I had no choice but to fight Gilbert Melendez for the Strikeforce lightweight championship on December 17, 2011. It was my shot at the belt and a ticket to the UFC. So I taped up my busted hand as best I could and went in there anyway. I really had a chance against Melendez. He had won and defended the lightweight title numerous times and went into that fight 19-2 and ranked No. 3 in the world. But I was still on the rise at 22-6 and No. 10 in the world.

You should see this fight for yourself. It's on YouTube. I can describe it, but you should see it. I went into the Octagon with the jacked-up right hand and hit Melendez with a right in the first round. I immediately backed off. *Fuck!* I had just fully destroyed the tendon; now I had a full-blown tear. I put my hands up, not to celebrate or taunt, but to shake it off. It looked like I was dancing around, but I was actually shaking my hand, trying not to show Melendez it was destroyed. I messed up his face and leg pretty badly in the fight. The dude couldn't walk the next day and I shut one of his eyes closed. I did well for having just one hand. While I didn't get my ass beat, I lost on a decision.

Had I won that fight, it would've changed my life. I'd have been ranked No. 1 or No. 2 in the world and gotten a shot at the UFC as a belt holder. That loss was devastating for my career and momentum. My ranking tanked into the twenties. Winning that belt meant fighting the UFC champ right away. Instead, I had to grind from the bottom to the top for years to get my ranking back. It's what I'd done my whole life, but this was different. I had gotten so close to my UFC dream. It would take years to regain my momentum after that loss.

I was depressed for a long time. I was a wreck: hand in a cast for months, unable to train. I put on weight, bills stacked up. I was depressed and anxious, feeling like I blew my one shot. I was stuck living in a shit-hole shack, just trying to feed my family.

The loss ate at me constantly for months. *What would have happened if I had my hand for that fight?* I wondered as I sat on the couch playing video games or lying awake at night. I know I would've won. I wouldn't have been sitting out seven months until my next fight. The anxiety raced through me; I thought I could change my life again and didn't.

I'd dropped the ball.

ROCK BOTTOM

I was crushed after I lost the Strikeforce title fight in 2012. If I had won that fight, I not only would have had the 155-pound belt but I'd have been fighting for the UFC belt next. Melendez fought one more time for Strikeforce and then signed on and challenged for the UFC lightweight title in his next fight. That could have been me if I'd won that night. That's what winning that lightweight belt meant. There was no way they could've denied me a title shot. I had beaten all the other top guys. I just didn't get it done against Melendez with my busted hand. I fell short. Losing that huge opportunity has eaten at me forever.

I had gotten an X-ray before the fight; it didn't show any broken bones. At the time, the doctors didn't think about getting an MRI so they could look at the ligaments. Nothing was broken, so I went to war. But afterward an orthopedic specialist said I'd torn my ligaments and fucked up my metacarpals. He wanted to do surgery but I wanted to avoid that at all costs. He put on a cast and we waited six weeks to allow it to heal. The doctor was shocked at the healing when they cut the cast off and said I could rehab it. I didn't know it was going to take a year and a half.

I did intensive rehab for months. But month after month it wasn't improving. As soon as I'd crack somebody, crazy pain. I could throw mean-ass combinations with my left hand, but as soon as my right hand touched anything, it fucking blew up. It wasn't even the pain; my hand would swell and go numb, and I'd get stingers from my fist all the way to my neck. I kept punching through it but was getting mixed opinions. The doctors told me it was my body telling me to stop, that if I wanted to get better I should stop immediately if it happened. On the other side of the coin, my fighting coaches were telling me to fucking push through that shit. "What the fuck is wrong with you?" they said. "You're being a fucking pussy." I was getting caught up in both worlds between listening to doctors or to coaches calling me weak. Between the busted hand and the uncertainty around the future, I fell into a deep depression.

With my hand screwed up, I couldn't fight or make money. I had my kids, so I'd wake up and take them to school. Then I'd go back home and hang around the house all day, eating junk food and playing video games: *Call of Duty, Street Fighter, Mortal Kombat*, more *Call of Duty*. Chasing girls was a big thing too. I had some money stashed away, so I used it to take off to Thailand for three weeks with some models while my baby mama and three-year-old daughter were at home. I came back to all my shit packed up and a letter calling me an asshole. She didn't even know about Thailand; she just found the girls I was texting on my phone. It was a mess.

I couldn't compete, so I tried working as a valet at a condo for quick cash. My friend said I'd make $300 a day on weekends. I figured I'd do that for ten weeks, save up all the money while my hand was fucked up, and then come back to fighting with some money. My friend had lied: I made like $25 the whole weekend.

I didn't talk to anybody about the depression or the dark place I had sunk into. Then one night, sitting on my couch, depressed, I smoked marijuana for the first time. I was at this low point, stressed about money and life, and the weed actually helped me see the world through a whole different lens. I had grown up around drug addicts and always thought potheads were lazy fucks. That wasn't me. I was a fucking go-getter. When I got high, I realized weed gave me an escape and released stress. At that time I didn't have an outlet or anyone to open up to. Weed helped pull me out of my funk and change my perspective, at least temporarily.

I did rehab hard for six months and nothing improved. By chance, I ended up teaching a seminar in Chile where this European doctor told me about ozone therapy and oxygen. He injected oxygen-ozone gas into my hand and it was like he gave it new life. I started doing ozone consistently and it really helped heal things up. My first fight back for Strikeforce was only six months after the title loss. My hand was still jacked up but I just got a cortisone shot to mask the pain and gutted out a split-decision win. But this ozone shit was a game-changer.

The guys at American Top Team were pivotal for my career. They always believed in me and gave me wisdom, direction, and positive reinforcement, even when I was fucking up. Dan and Paulino, especially, would check me when I was partying too hard and slacking on training and diet after the injury. They knew I was a wild man with self-destructive tendencies from my upbringing in the streets, so they'd quickly get on me. "Hey, that's cool and all, but you do have a career," they'd tell me, "and that career is your body being at its top peak." My eating habits were poor and I didn't take care of myself, especially after messing up my hand. I'd just be out partying all the time. And Dan and Paulino would warn me, "You're throwing away your gifts."

In the spring of 2011, the UFC bought Strikeforce and all the fighters' contracts. Months went by after the purchase and I wasn't getting offered any fights. Lower-ranked guys were getting fights because the UFC wanted to build up their fighters by giving them favorable matchups against Strikeforce guys. Guys ranked No. 7 or No. 8 were fighting the UFC's No. 2 and No. 3. Those were the kind of top-contender fights I should've been getting. I didn't understand it. I went 5-1 in Strikeforce; I was their second- or third-best lightweight. My only loss there was a close decision to the champion in a five-round fight with a fucked-up right hand. I felt like the UFC was shelving me while other guys leapfrogged ahead. It was bullshit.

I was healthy and ready to go, but the UFC just didn't want to put me on a card. They were making it really difficult for me to get fights. I'd had enough. I was ready to go stand on a street corner in Miami with a sign to call them out. My friends suggested I just take the picture in the gym and post it online instead. Fuck it. I grabbed a piece of paper and a Sharpie and wrote: HUNGRY!! WILL FIGHT FOR FOOD!! BACK-YARDS, UFC, KFC. SHOW ME THE $$$!!!

I wasn't going to sit back quietly and get shelved.

Young Jorge

Tita and Papa Dukes

Jorge and Mama Dukes

Stepdad Julio, Jorge, Mama Dukes, Tia Norma

Jorge, Mama Dukes

Paulino and Jorge

Jorge and Yoel Romero

Paulino, Jorge, Dylan Capetillo, Fernando Vargas Jr.,
and Jorge Capetillo

USS *Farragut*
sailor and Jorge

Jorge and President Trump

CHAPTER 10

FIGHTING FOR A SHOT

After the UFC bought StrikeForce, swallowed it up, and absorbed all the fighters' contracts into the UFC, it was a mess. I fought three more times for Strikeforce between June 2011 and July 2012, but then it went quiet. I was twenty-eight, couldn't get a fight, and was low on cash. I was staying on my buddy Ike's couch in Miami. All those years later and I was still couch surfing. Ike was a major MMA nerd—ran his own website and shit—so we'd spend hours scrolling through forums, reading up on the latest UFC gossip and news.

At the end of 2012, after multiple Strikeforce fight weekends were canceled because of tensions, word came out that the UFC was going to fold the Strikeforce promotion altogether. I hadn't fought in nearly six months and was still waiting to see what the UFC was going to do with my contract. Was I ever going to get a UFC fight? What happened when Strikeforce folded?

One day in January 2013, we were sitting there when Ike perked up. Ike was a wizard at finding insider info on underground forums and had stumbled on a leaked list of Strikeforce fighters the UFC was putting on upcoming cards. My heart started racing. This could be huge.

I rushed over to check that shit out. We frantically scrolled through the list of names. My eyes darted up and down as the list rolled by, searching for one name: Masvidal. I couldn't spot it. We kept scrolling and scrolling. Still nothing. No fucking Masvidal anywhere. I felt my stomach drop. *What the fuck?* I thought. *I hope this ain't true.* The UFC denied the list's legitimacy and said it wasn't real. But when it finally came out not long after, it was official. My name was nowhere on it.

I was fucking devastated. I sunk deeper into a seriously dark place. I just couldn't stop thinking about that Strikeforce title bout loss the year before. If I'd won that Strikeforce belt, I'd be going to the UFC as the lightweight champ. But now I had to start over from the bottom. The UFC owned my contract but they weren't offering me fights. I saw other guys I'd beaten getting spots. It was bullshit. I finished fights, I was exciting, I'd throw down anytime, anywhere. But for some reason the UFC wasn't giving me a chance.

Throughout my career up until that point, it always seemed like the UFC liked me and didn't at the same time. Over the years the UFC dangled lowball contract offers, even when I was fighting for other promotions like Bellator and Strikeforce. I was beating their former fighters left and right, knocking dudes out who had been in the UFC. But they kept tossing me weak deals. So I said, *Screw it*, went and fought for Bodog in Costa Rica and Russia in 2006, and took the five fights in Japan after that. I went all over—everywhere else except the UFC.

Now I was *in* the UFC—at least, they owned my contract—and I still couldn't get a fight. Was it my reputation? I didn't fucking know. Maybe it was because of the "thug" label from the backyard fights. The media was always labeling me a street thug because of that shit, calling me a journeyman already when I was twenty-three. After losses early in my career, there were people on websites saying, "Street thug fighter loses title bout," or "Back to the streets for him." All because of some backyard throw downs when I was younger. That street fighter tag stuck with me but it wasn't everything I was. Yeah, I had started fighting in the streets, but I busted my ass to be a real prizefighter, not just some brawler. Fighting was my whole life, from sunup to sundown. If I wasn't in the gym training, I was studying tapes, reading books, and talking techniques with coaches or other fighters. My brain was completely immersed. I lived and died by the gym. Street fighting wasn't my life or my end goal. My goal was to hold a UFC championship belt, and street fighting was the means to do that. The media could call me a thug and street fighter—they could call me whatever the fuck they wanted—but nothing was going to stop me from proving I was a legit prizefighter who could hang at the highest level.

I was always professional as I moved from promotion to promotion. I never missed weight or failed a drug test once in my career—something a lot of fighters can't say. I put in the work to be on time, make weight, and bring my A game to every fight. But still, the UFC dragged their feet when it came to me. It was confusing why the UFC seemed to be dogging me and making me wait so long for a fight when I did things the right way.

The months passed with no call from the UFC. I made some noise with my street sign, but it still took time. Seven agonizing months went by after my last Strikeforce fight. Then finally my phone buzzed one day with a text.

ENTERING THE OCTAGON

I was in a casino on a reservation somewhere in California—fuck if I remember the name—gambling and cornering a buddy in a fight they had going on there when I get a text from Dan Lambert: "Hey, I think you got a fight, but it's a tough one. I don't know if you're gonna want to take it, man."

Dan knew I'd never turn down a fight, so he was trolling, building up this guy like he was the boogeyman. "This guy's good," he said. "He's on a big win streak, but if you could beat this guy, you'll be on a good fucking path." I didn't give a damn who it was. After waiting so long, I was ready to throw down with anyone. "Yeah, whatever the fuck, bro," I said. "How long do I have to prepare? I'm gonna kick this guy's ass."

All I needed to know was when and where. I was already helping a couple of guys prepare for fights, so I was in decent shape. They gave me eight weeks to ramp up. My first thought? *I'm gonna fucking beat the fuck out of this guy.* I knew I would put on a show and beat this guy, whoever he was. Didn't matter: on that UFC stage, I was going to showcase what I could do. I had been fighting professionally since I was eighteen and had waited ten years for this moment. I was more than ready to put on a show for the world.

The money wasn't much more than I was already making. I had gotten $26,000 to show and $26,000 to win in my last Strikeforce fight; the UFC was paying me $33,000 and $33,000 or something like that for my debut. But as money hungry as I am, it wasn't about that. It was about finally getting that shot in the big show—about proving I deserved to be there with the best.

Get this shit: the card I made my UFC debut on was headlined by Gilbert Melendez, who was making his UFC debut for the UFC light-weight championship. How fucking ironic. I was the lead-in to the guy who took the Strikeforce title from me. As if it hadn't eaten at me enough, it was another reminder that if I'd won that fight, I could've been the main event on this card, fighting for a title.

Whatever. I was booked against Tim Means—not a huge name but a dangerous up-and-comer. The dude was 18-3-1, on a nine-fight winning streak, and only lost once in his previous 18 fights. What made Means tricky was he was a six-foot-two southpaw fighting at 155 pounds. With his height, he was awkward and lanky for a lightweight.

I remember Means being an unpredictable striker. At his height he had a huge reach advantage: we're talking seven, eight inches over the average lightweight. He could knee and elbow from angles you didn't expect. The dude was crafty with his stand-up. Means had this long undefeated streak earlier in his career until he got locked up. After jail, he got clean, turned his life around, and was rolling by the time we fought. Nobody—I mean nobody—wanted to fight this guy because he was so dangerous. But I never shied away from a scrap.

I wasn't nervous when I walked out of the tunnel, but I definitely had some jitters. They call them the "Octagon jitters." Shit, I had some; I won't lie. The crowd, the lights, the whole scene—it's amped-up in the UFC. There are Octagon girls circling in bikinis, the emcee hyping up the crowd between fights, flashing lights, and rock music. You felt like you were the main attraction, with the cameras zooming in on your face as you made that walk to an arena filled with 15,000 screaming fans. It's an electric, surreal feeling you have to experience yourself to really understand. Other promotions were small-time compared to the spectacle of a UFC event. And everything moves differently compared to other promotions. Five minutes means five minutes. When they tell you you're on deck, get ready, because it's go time. The UFC was big-time.

Fighting is fighting. But the UFC is different. There's a reason when people say "the Octagon," it stands alone without explanation. I was used to fighting in Bellator's thirty-six-foot circle cage and Strikeforce's hexagonal cage in other promotions. The UFC uses an eight-sided caged ring, the aptly named and instantly recognizable thirty-foot "octagon." At twenty-eight years old and after thirty professional MMA fights across nearly ten years, I was finally going to step into the Octagon.

With Means, I knew I couldn't just stand and trade punches. He had too much reach and threw crazy strikes and elbows. I planned to go on the offensive with my wrestling, take him down, and neutralize his stand-up. I started out landing combos, mixing in body kicks and right hands in the first round, but I kept my focus on securing take-downs. It was a back-and-forth struggle, but I managed to get him to the mat and wrestle him. It was one of the only times in my career I leaned on my grappling. I dominated the fight with my control and takedowns—and left with a unanimous decision.

Bleacher Report wrote after the fight: "If this fight is remembered for anything, it will be remembered as the launching point of Masvidal's UFC career." Damn straight. It wasn't my best performance, maybe a 5 or 6 out of 10. But it was a solid start. I'd come a long way from watching bootleg UFC at my buddy's crib growing up. This was just the beginning. That 2013 win finally helped me land on more UFC cards, but the UFC didn't give me any top-ranked guys for years. If I was going to make a name, I had to grind from the very bottom up.

MOVING ON UP

After I beat Means, the UFC started offering me more fights. I fought two more times that same year in 2013 and three more in 2014. By the end of my second full year in the UFC, I had gone 5-1. Going into 2015, I was riding high on a three-fight win streak—unanimous decisions against Pat Healy, Daron Cruickshank, and James Krause—that put me on the doorstep of a lightweight title shot. In my mind, I was only one big win away. When the UFC offered me Al Iaquinta, I saw the perfect opportunity to kick that door down. In the lightweight rankings, he was No. 9 after a trio of knockout wins, while I was sitting at No. 14. I knew that if I could get past Iaquinta decisively, I'd be making my case for a championship bout.

I went into the fight looking to make a statement. As soon as the opening bell rang, I stepped on the gas and went right after Iaquinta, establishing my jab and lighting him up. I exploded forward with a jumping knee that landed flush and hurt him. I could see his legs wobble as I cracked him with a body kick and a quick combination. Sure enough, he shot in desperately for a takedown, but I stuffed it and made him pay, dropping punches and elbows as the round ended with him on the ground and me in total control.

Round two was closer. Iaquinta focused on hitting me with body shots while failing to get me to the mat. But my left hook kept finding his face. Even though my right eye was swelling, I never felt truly threatened. Heading into the third, I knew I was up two rounds to none. I have to give Iaquinta credit: he poured pressure on in the final round, attacking my leg as he tried to steal the fight. But I kept cracking him every time he got close. As the final seconds ticked off, I felt I had clearly won the first two rounds, even if the third was tighter.

So when Bruce Buffer announced a split decision, I was fucking stunned. I patted Iaquinta on the back and walked out of the Octagon shaking my head in disbelief. The stats, the fans, and the media—they all backed me up. I felt robbed.

I out-landed him 83 to 55 in total strikes.

I crushed him 62 to 18 in head strikes.

I never got taken down.

The crowd booed him immediately, pissing Iaquinta off. "Are you booing me?" he said. "You better not boo me! I fucking fought my ass off! Fuck you!" He walked out. Sherdog named the fight the 2015 Robbery of the Year, but that didn't change the result. I didn't want a rematch. As far as I was concerned, I won that fight.

SO CLOSE, YET SO FAR

With the UFC planning to ban IV rehydration treatments at the end of 2015, I knew my days draining myself to make the cut at lightweight were numbered. I struggled badly in those weight cuts, and Paulino was right: after draining my body to get to 155, I was never physically the same fighter on fight night. Losing IVs was the final straw for me.

After the Iaquinta debacle, the UFC offered me Cezar Ferreira for my welterweight debut. He was dropping down from 185 while I moved up to 170. I'd be giving up some size to the six-foot-one Brazilian, but I didn't give a shit: I wanted to see what I could do against the bigger guys at welterweight.

That fight week was completely different from my first seven in the UFC. My speed and reflexes felt like my old self again. I could eat real food and not obsess over making weight. On weigh-in day I actually came in slightly overweight after being tempted by In-N-Out Burger earlier that week. Whoops. I sweated off the two pounds and made it. By fight night I knew I was primed to make a statement. I woke up feeling fast and strong—none of the usual brain fog or sluggishness that had plagued my previous camps.

My two losses at lightweight were still fresh wounds; both came at the hands of the judges. After feeling that another fight was stolen from me on the scorecards against Iaquinta, I was done leaving my fate to the three people sitting cageside. Ferreira was getting finished.

Ferreira came out aggressive, hitting me with kicks and punches as we felt each other out. He shot in and momentarily took my back. But I got up quickly to avoid any real danger. Then suddenly everything clicked. I exploded with a lethal elbow that buckled him. I could see he was on shaky legs, and I poured it on with four booming follow-up punches that put him down hard. A few final shots on the mat sealed the deal. With the TKO victory in the first round, I had officially arrived at welterweight in brutal fashion. No playing it safe.

I had demonstrated my ability in a new weight class, but I still had plenty left in the tank. I called out the top contenders in my post-fight interview, letting the welterweight division know I was gunning straight for the top. I'd fight anyone they put in front of me. I wanted ranked competition, end of story.

The UFC listened. After eight fights and over two years, I was finally offered a main event: "UFC Fight Night: Henderson vs. Masvidal." It wasn't a shock at all, just reassurance of what I always knew would happen. I envisioned myself headlining cards, selling pay-per-views, breaking records, knocking dudes out, becoming a world champ. Every time a big moment like that happened, I had already envisioned it a million times. It might sound cocky, but it's the honest truth. With all the blood and sweat I put in, it wasn't an "if" but a "when" in my mind. I 100 percent expected it. Even when I wasn't the best fighter, I was busting my ass. I had a great eye for the sport from training with killers and world champions across weight classes at American Top Team, so I knew I could beat a lot of the top guys. It was about fucking time.

That card brought everything full circle. Benson Henderson had won the UFC lightweight belt against Melendez two years earlier as the main event on the card where I had made my UFC debut. He'd lost it since and we had both recently moved up to welterweight, but he was No. 10 in the division. Now I had the chance to go to South Korea and beat his ass.

For weeks I was actually scheduled to fight Dong Hyun Kim in South Korea. But two weeks out from the event, the other headliner, Thiago Alves, got hurt. They moved me up to headline against Henderson—not just a higher-ranked opponent, but a five-round fight instead of three. That was where I was banking on the extra energy to pay off at 170 pounds.

I came out landing punches against Henderson and won the first round on the scorecards. In the second round, Henderson picked up the pace and started going for takedowns, eventually trapping me against the fence with a flying knee in the fourth. In the fifth, I almost secured a standing guillotine choke near the fence, but he fell backward and eventually escaped. I just missed it.

I swear I beat Henderson's ass in that fight. If you watch it, you'd be amazed I took it on fourteen days' notice and went five rounds with that animal. I walked him down and beat the fuck out of him. But I lost a split decision: one judge had me winning, one had Henderson, and the decider went to Henderson. I came so close to winning that main event. A few things go differently and it's my hand in the air. I wish I had more time to prep for the five rounds, but that's the nature of the beast. I showed my evolution from undercard veteran to going twenty-five minutes for the main event. It wasn't my time yet, but I left no doubt I belonged at that top level.

For years the UFC just wouldn't give me ranked fights, and every time they did only begrudgingly, my opponent would get snatched up to fight someone else instead. It wasn't until somebody got hurt and I stepped in on two weeks' notice, going from a three-round fight to a five-round fight in South Korea, that the UFC started giving me ranked fights. I notched three more wins over the next year or so after the Henderson main event, but two losses and injuries in 2017 began to derail my career. As I healed up, I couldn't get a fight booked.

My UFC record had fallen to 9-6, so I didn't have a massive name or big ranking. But skillwise I was still dangerous. The top guys didn't want to risk fighting me. They had seen what I'd done to Henderson on short notice. I was kind of getting ducked, and when I was offered a fight, it was only guys outside the top ten. Nothing made sense for me. I was too far in my career for scrubs but couldn't get bigger names to sign up. As one month without a fight became six, I found myself at another frustrating crossroads, trying to keep my UFC dream alive.

CHAPTER 11

EXATLÓN

Fuck Abe, I thought as I lay under the bed. *He wouldn't take no for an answer and now I'm under some random grandma's bed listening to guys raid the village, looking for me. If I make it out of here, I'm going to kill him.*

Earlier in 2018, I was sitting on my couch one day, coming off two consecutive frustrating losses and waiting for my injuries to heal. I kept saying publicly, "I'm gonna fight. I'm gonna fight," but I wasn't telling anybody when. My career was at a frustrating standstill. After fifteen long years and forty-five fights, I was still searching for that breakthrough moment. Everyone was trying to help me crack the code, but only I held the answer. All I knew was that at thirty-three years old, I felt my time was limited.

As I stared blankly at the TV, my phone rang. It was my manager, Abraham Kawa. He was calling for our usual check-in about potential fights.

"Hey, man," he said. "I got this opportunity."

"What's going on with the fights," I asked. "You heard anything?"

"No," he said. "But I got this reality show."

I paused, not sure I heard him right. "Say that again?"

"I got this reality show," he repeated.

Click. I hung up without saying another word. He called back and I let it go to voicemail. He left a message begging me to reconsider. This reality show *Exatlón* had called Abe and wanted me to be a contestant on the first season of the show. I had zero interest in some silly show.

My focus was getting back in the Octagon after two setbacks the year before, in 2017. At that point in my fighting career, I was at a crossroads after a pair of letdowns. There was a point, from July 2016 to January 2017, where I won three straight bouts on UFC cards. Ross Pearson, Jake Ellenberger, Donald Cerrone. Boom. Boom. Boom. Two of them I knocked out cold. I'd done enough to bounce back from that South Korea loss to Henderson and get a UFC welterweight title eliminator match against Demian Maia. I was inching toward another chance at a belt, this time in the UFC. I just needed to beat Maia at UFC 211.

He had a tricky jujitsu game and—stubborn me—I decided to try to fight his strengths instead of sticking to my game plan. I'd made that mistake before: trying to beat specialists at their game out of stubbornness. If somebody was known as a good jujitsu guy, I was going to out-jujitsu that guy instead of doing what I needed to do to beat him. I always wanted to be better than somebody else at their thing, which led to a lot of letdowns. And that's what happened against Maia. I lost another close split decision because I was too focused on showing I could beat him at his game rather than just taking him out. My coaches tried to get through to me, but at that point in my career I thought I knew better. I was too hardheaded to take their advice and stick to my strengths.

I was so close—one win away from fighting for the UFC championship match. But I came up short yet again at the worst possible time. Losing that split decision was crushing. If I had won that eliminator bout, I would have fought Tyron Woodley for the welterweight title. We had been teammates at American Top Team, so I was confident I could have beaten him in a title fight. It would have been a good matchup for me because Woodley was more of a striker than a wrestler. But the Maia loss slammed that door shut.

That post-fight locker room with Dan, my coach Mike Brown, and American Top Team general manager Richie Guerriero was one of the most depressing locker rooms I've ever been in. I'd lost before, but this one hurt. I had my shot to break through after all those years of blood and sweat. And I didn't cross the bridge. To sit there again on my journey with another split decision? *Fuck!* Nearing my mid-thirties, I saw my potential going to waste. I had beaten world champions and ranked guys. But I wasn't a young prospect anymore. I didn't know how many more chances I'd get and I was nowhere near where I wanted to be. Another devastating setback when I was right there within reach of achieving my ultimate dream. There was a lot of uncertainty.

Around then, Leon Edwards, a twentysomething fighter looking to make a name for himself, called me out after beating Cerrone via unanimous decision. I had knocked Cerrone out a few UFC cards earlier, so I guess Edwards wanted a piece of me. "Me and Masvidal, let's go. Let's make it happen," Edwards told the world from the Octagon. "I like to take out the old guns. Masvidal, he's been around a long time, so why not go in there and take him out?"

Fuck, other fighters were always calling me out. I didn't give two shits who called me out; I just wanted a big fight. I'd just had a call with the UFC asking for fights but kept getting turned down. Darren Till was waiting for a title shot. Rafael dos Anjos, Kamaru Usman, and Neil Magny weren't interested. I tried to get rematches with Maia and Stephen Thompson, who I'd lost to at the end of 2017, but no go. The rest of the top ten were booked up, injured, or ducking me. At thirty-three and ranked No. 8, I only wanted the top ten guys. Or at least someone to inch me toward the title. Edwards wasn't on my level. When Edwards called me out, he wasn't even in the top twenty. But at that point a fight was a fight. Beggars can't be choosers. I couldn't keep waiting for fantasy matchups that were never going to happen. But it turned out Edwards was all talk. That matchup never happened either.

A few months passed, and I was getting healthier and restless sitting around. I called Abe, told him I'd be ready to fight soon, and asked if he'd heard anything new.

"No, I haven't," he said. "I only got this." He started listing fighters who were willing to fight.

Only crap matchups.

"That's shit," I told him. "No, fuck those guys." I wasn't going to fight just anybody. I didn't want to look desperate.

"Well," he said, "I got the reality show."

Click. I hung up.

This is what I'm paying him for? Some fucking Jersey Shore *shit?* I thought. Not a chance. As I was telling him no and sending him to go fuck himself, he was doing the same thing on the other end, telling *Exatlón*, "Not a chance. He's not gonna do it." They were relentless with their recruitment. I must have hung up on Abe three different times. It sounded like *The Real World* or some shit. I wanted no part of it.

More time passed and I called Abe back, frustrated.

"Hey," I said. "I'm broke. It's been, like, eight months. I'm pretty healed up. We need to fight."

"Okay, this is what I got on the table," he said.

More shitty fighters. Nobody in the top ten.

"Since you said no so much to the reality show, they upped the price," Abe said. "Let me explain before you hang up. It's not what you think."

Abe started breaking down what *Exatlón* was. It was like if *American Ninja Warrior* and *Survivor* had a baby. I was being recruited to compete on the first season of *Exatlón United States* on Telemundo, but the series had several different seasons with people from all over: *Exatlón México*, *Exatlón Colombia*, and so on. One team was a "celebrity" team made up of athletes and celebrities: Olympians, gymnasts, fighters, soccer players, you name it. The other teams were the "contenders," made up of influencers and up-and-coming athletes. Each team had five men and five women competing in physical and mental challenges for basic needs and survival.

On the show, there was no TV, no cell phones, no outside contact. You were isolated in the jungles in the Dominican Republic. Throughout the week there were team battles over living conditions, then on Sunday there was an elimination to kick someone off from the losing team. The winning team lived in a big house with AC and hot water and ate like kings, feasting on lobster and steak. The losing team lived in a wooden shack with barely running water, slept on little thin mattresses thrown on the floor, and ate rice and fish. The last person standing in the finale won $200,000. Plus they made me a good offer just to show up and compete. Win or lose, I was going to get paid a very handsome weekly fee.

I'd never seen the show, but it was enough money to make me reconsider. I didn't know what I was getting myself into, but I wasn't getting any good fights from the UFC and still wasn't in the best shape, so I said, "Fuck it, I'll go on this reality show for a few weeks and grab a couple of paychecks." My time off was getting long, so maybe this would hold me over until I could get back in the Octagon.

A FIGHTING MINDSET

From a young age I had always been that kind of guy with a million questions buzzing around in his head. It's like there was this constant thirst for understanding the inner workings of a fighter's mind right before they step into the ring. Are they raging with anger? Or are they calm and collected? I knew fighting wasn't just about stepping into the cage and throwing hands. It's about what's going on up here, in your mind, right before you go out there to perform. What's the mindset of the great competitors? I was always eager to learn.

When *Exatlón* came calling, promising some serious cash, I thought, *Hell, why not?* I signed up to be on the red team, the celebrity squad, pitted against the up-and-coming blue team. Our red team was packed with an impressive roster of athletes. There was Marisela Cantú, an Olympic gymnast from Mexico; Leonel Manzano, a runner who had snagged a silver medal in the mile for the U.S. at the 2012 Olympics; and Tommy Ramos, an Olympic gymnast for Puerto Rico. On top of that, we had standout soccer players and CrossFit trainers and champions. I was surrounded by all these different talented athletes. The main draw for me was the money—as it was often in my career—but it didn't take long after I arrived in the Dominican Republic to realize these world-class athletes could teach me a thing or two.

I never played sports growing up. No basketball, football, soccer, baseball, nothing. My whole life was fighting. I didn't know how to throw a football or shoot a basketball. I had a lot of athletic ability, but stamina or punches didn't translate to those sports. So when I landed in the Dominican Republic and joined *Exatlón*, it was like stepping into a whole new world. I was starting from scratch with a shit ton to learn. I had to outwork the other competitors because I was the worst at just about everything when I started.

The early days for the red team were rough. We were getting our asses handed to us by the up-and-comers. They weren't well-known but they were still great competitors, including parkour athletes and minor-league baseball players who were eager to prove themselves. For the first several weeks, they were kicking everybody's ass, which meant my survival was constantly on the line. Every Sunday, the two worst performers on the losing team faced elimination. Shit, I found myself in that position almost every week for the first six weeks.

The one thing that played to my advantage on elimination Sundays was the obstacle course and target-shooting challenge. It was a best-of-seven showdown, and the two players up for elimination had to win four games to stay. That meant we were going to have to run the track at least four times. That wasn't a problem for me. I might not be the fastest guy, but I sure as hell wasn't going to tire out. When I reached the finish line, my heart was pounding, but I had the experience of working under that kind of pressure. It was like going five rounds in a fight: you had to have enough left physically and mentally at the end. I had worked under those conditions my entire life. Plus I still had energy left to spare. All we ever had to eat were coconuts. Breakfast, lunch, and dinner. When we lost, which was happening a lot at that time, all we got from the show was a bowl of rice and two slices of pineapple, so I was constantly scrounging up the coconuts from the trees. They were our lifeline. Once I got the hang of shooting targets, I started knocking guys out during eliminations, week after week. I was the survivor.

Each week that I survived meant more time for me to tap into the brains of my teammates. Manzano, who ran a four-minute mile or something fucking outrageous, became my go-to guy. He showed me workouts, how to run, how to pace myself, and even different breathing techniques. Other athletes on the team taught me the details of their sports, like ab workouts and how they engaged their cores. It was like an education in elite-level sports. I absorbed everything I could. Before long I started getting the hang of the different sports. My skills were improving and I thought, *Maybe I can fucking win this thing.* Once that thought got in my head, there was no stopping me. I was in it to win it. The experience ended up teaching me way more than I expected.

THE MENTAL GAME

The Dominican Republic was unlike any place I'd ever experienced. The jungle where we were stationed covered twenty acres, deep in the mountainous Las Terrenas on the Samaná Peninsula. The mountains bridged the gap between the beach and dense forest. It was a surreal experience, being smack dab in the middle of nowhere, with the whitest sand you could ever imagine just a thousand feet away. It was just the ten of us from the red team; the blue team was in another fucking dimension for all we knew.

Every day I found myself alone deep in the jungle, surrounded by towering palm trees. The stark contrast between the jungle and the beach was like a scene out of a movie. One moment you're hacking through vines, and the next you're dipping your feet in the ocean. It was like paradise.

It was in that Dominican jungle where I had an epiphany that changed the game for me. I thank God to this day that it happened there, in the midst of the jungle, and not in a jail cell or a hospital bed. I was alone, cut off from the world, with hardly any food and only my thoughts for company. And let me tell you, it was the best isolation I've ever experienced.

I had almost three and a half decades of data on my life and career. I was truly alone, cut off from the noise and chaos of the world. It was in that silence and isolation that my thoughts began to take shape, sparking revelations that would reshape my life. That was the perfect setting for introspection and a moment of clarity. I started diving deep into my personal and professional life, connecting the dots between my victories and my losses, unraveling what worked and what didn't.

I questioned everything, examined my successes, and analyzed my failures. What had I done right and wrong in those defining moments? When I'd knocked out an opponent, what had been the recipe for my success? How did I train, what did I eat, and how did I prepare? I hadn't been consistent in my approach; there were moments when I'd let loose like a maniac and others when I kept my control. I tried to unravel the mysteries and unlock the secrets of my own potential. It was all about identifying patterns, understanding my own strengths and weaknesses, and finding the winning formula. By that point in my life I knew two things for sure. First, I had all the essential ingredients to be a fighter: speed, power, reflexes, durability. I checked off all the boxes. Second, I was fucking tough as hell. I had won so many fights through sheer toughness. It was clear I had what it took, but I needed to refine my approach, avoid getting trapped in an opponent's specialty, and carve my own path to victory. I had accumulated fifteen years of data in the cage, but I had never taken the time to analyze it. It was only in the solitude of that Dominican jungle that I started connecting the dots.

During my free time on the show, I was constantly alone, spending my days in solitary reflection. There was a particular mountain I often climbed, and I'd get better and faster each time. In the beginning, it took me thirty minutes, but I eventually cut it down to just ten. Although security guards usually accompanied the contestants everywhere, they'd let me go alone. It was grueling, and not many could keep up. Plus there were challenges beyond the climb. The jungle was filled with recluse spiders, snakes, and fucking ticks. But the real nightmare was the centipedes. Everybody told me if they stung you, you'd get a two-week fever and it hurt like fucking hell. Every time I'd make that trek, I'd make damn sure I was covered up from head to toe, chopping my way down through the mountain. So the security guards were fine letting me be alone, knowing I always came down. At the peak of the mountain, I was in a world of my own. I could see what felt like the entire Dominican Republic, from the beach to a hundred miles in every direction. I'd go up there to pray and think. It was an epic view, especially during sunrise and sunset. The isolation, for me, was crucial. I had never realized it before, but I needed that time to be alone with my thoughts, my feelings, with whatever was going on in my head.

When I first joined *Exatlón*, I had a recurring apprehension. *Maybe I'm done fighting. Fuck, what do I do?* Injuries, a lack of big-time fights despite beating some great fighters—all these uncertainties clouded my mind during my time in the Dominican jungle, with no music, no TV, and no friends to talk to. Nobody called me in the middle of the night drunkenly looking for a ride; there were no distractions to pull me away. While there were other people on the show, most of my hours were spent alone because my teammates weren't getting lost in the jungle like I was. I would trek deep into the jungle for hours on end—sometimes four, other times six—returning with bags I'd filled with fruit along the way. I'd lose myself in the dense forest, not worrying about getting lost.

As I wandered through the wilderness day after day and week after week, I started having a different perspective: *I still want to fight. I still have things to do.* It was a whisper that grew into something more. I knew without a doubt that I wasn't ready to hang up the gloves. I had more to give, more to prove, and more fights to win. Sure, I was thirty-three years old. But my journey wasn't over; it was just beginning.

That pivotal realization might have slipped through my fingers forever if I had hung up on Abe one more time. Where would my career have gone if I hadn't trekked into the heart of that jungle, far away from all the noise and chaos of my everyday life? Fighting had been in my blood for as long as I could remember, but it always had to share its space. I'd scrap both inside and outside the cage, hustling to make ends meet, doing whatever it took to provide for myself and the people I cared about. It's not that fighting didn't rule a big part of my world, but it wasn't the only game in town.

After three months in the Dominican Republic, I was standing on the edge of a new beginning. My dedication to the fight game was unwavering and my focus was laser-sharp. I was ready to take all the wisdom I had picked up and apply it to my career. The fighting chapter of my life wasn't over. I was just getting started.

CHAPTER 12

ESCAPE

The Turkish production company that ran all of the *Exatlón* shows had taken over a huge plot of rural Dominican Republic to film. They controlled the entire area and made it feel like a prison with all their rules and surveillance. It was their show, their rules, and they enforced them like wardens.

The security guards were the real foot soldiers of *Exatlón*. They worked grueling twelve-hour shifts, day in and day out, making maybe $400 or $600 a month. For them, their jobs were everything. They couldn't risk losing them, so they were watching us constantly. It was like a never-ending game of cat and mouse. While we were out there playing the show's games, the security guards were back at our camp ransacking our bags, searching for contraband. The show was strict on outside contraband. No weed, no chocolate, no coffee, no Coca-Cola—you name it, it was off-limits.

If the security crew found something as they looked through our bags, it was game on. Find a phone number and they'd dial it up. "Omar had a phone number in here. Who is this? Call it up." They'd call and a security guard on the show would answer. They'd bring the guard in to interrogate them. "Why does he have your fucking number? Why the fuck are you talking to him?" Fired. The show producers didn't want to take any chance of cheating.

They had a lot of rules and I had always had a problem with authority. So as you might have guessed, I was a problem on *Exatlón*. It took me a minute to figure out how to work the system, but as the first days and weeks passed I started noticing who the real players were behind the scenes, calling the shots. The security guards were locals, so they came and went. Eventually I got friendly with one of the security guys, joking around whenever we crossed paths. We weren't allowed to have money on the show, so to get some I gave the guard my friend's Instagram and had him hit him up for a transfer. The thing was, my friend had a common name, and when the guard looked it up, seven profiles showed up. "Listen," I told him, "message all seven of them. One of them's gotta be him." Finally we narrowed it down. "Okay," I said, "tell him you need two hundred dollars from Masvidal." I even sent him a voice note, jokingly pleading, "These motherfuckers got me hostage here. I need a grand or they're gonna kill me." The problem? My friend believed it and didn't know what to do. He freaked out, didn't answer his phone, and vanished for a week. I was thinking, *What the fuck, man? This is my guy.* It took a week, but we finally talked to him. "I thought it was real," he said. "I didn't know what to do." I told him, "Bro, no, I was joking, but I do need this money." So he sent the security guard $200 through Caribbean Express. I told the security guard to keep $50 for himself and gave him a list of what I needed, and he brought me almost all the shit I was craving.

Imagine: there was no sugar, no coffee, no Coca-Cola, no chocolate. None of that shit. Now I was the guy who had everything. I had the weed, I had the jars of Nutella, I was the one with the Coca-Cola. Most of my teammates didn't know because I didn't offer it to anyone. I had a close little crew of teammates, so after dinner I'd signal them and we'd sneak into the forest because they had cameras in the house and everywhere around it. We'd make sure there were no security guards around. My guard would leave the delivery on a rock some-where. It sounds fucking crazy, but it's the truth. Nutella and slices of bread waiting for us.

"Look what I got, guys," I'd tell them.

"How the hell did you get that?" they'd asked.

"Don't even sweat it," I'd say, "just enjoy it."

We'd eat an entire jar of Nutella in one night, it was so damn good. There were four of us that were close. So I'd hook us up.

The showrunners hated me because I was pulling all this off under their noses. They started catching on to all the crazy shit I was pulling. *Wait a second*, they must've thought, *how is this guy getting all this contra-band in here?* I'd take off into the jungle to escape whenever they were after me. Every time I thought I'd finally lost the guards, thinking I'd gone so fucking far, they'd pop up, like, *Bro, what are you doing? Let's go!* I'd think, *Fuck, bro.* I'd been running in one direction for an hour, and somehow they'd still catch me. That was crazy.

Exatlón was a test of survival on more fronts than one: a game within a game, a mental test, and a gamble of risks and rewards. As I schemed and played the system, I found myself in week thirteen and the game was starting to wear on me. The isolation had its appeal and it had given me renewed purpose. It had been nearly a year since I'd stepped into the Octagon. My family, the adrenaline of fighting—they were calling my name. It was time to find a way out, a way back to the life I'd left behind.

THE GREAT ESCAPE

My daughter's birthday was a week away, and three months of separation was beginning to eat at me. When I first signed up for *Exatlón* in July

2018, I made sure there was an exemption in my contract so I could go home for her birthday on October 6 if I lasted that long on the show. I'd do the show, but I needed that one day. They agreed. I would come and compete in the show, and if I happened to still be around, they'd send me home for a day. I wasn't even sure I'd make it twelve weeks, but, sure enough, I was still there as the date approached.

I approached the producers, but instead of simply letting me go for the day, they turned it into a competition. It would no longer be a simple visit. The red team would face off against the blue team, competing for the privilege to see their kids. It was a game to them, a plot twist in their show. "You guys told me that no matter what happened, I'd go fucking see my kids," I protested. "You guys fucking promised me that." I was furious. *Fuck them!* I told them I wasn't going to compete in their stupid show. They begged me. "Listen, we'll take care of you no matter what," they said. "Just compete. Do it for the cameras." I caved, took their word for it, and did the show.

I was stressed competing with so much on the line. We had to do these puzzle block brainteasers at the end, which I fucking suck at. My adrenaline was pumping; I wanted to go-go-go—run, throw a football, or do some other shit—not do some fucking riddle. I bombed and we lost. Afterward I asked the production people when I was heading home. "We spoke with the crew and you can't go," they said. "It wouldn't be fair to the others. You're not the only one with kids." I exploded. This wasn't what we had agreed upon. I made a dash for it, sprinting into the jungle. We had signed something saying we owed $100,000 if we escaped, but, hey, I didn't have a dollar to my name. *Where are they gonna get it from?* I thought. *Fuck these guys.* I was back alone in the jungle, set on getting to town and getting out. But they had eyes everywhere. Within ninety minutes, a group of twenty-five guards on motorcycles had closed in on me.

After the guards caught me and returned me to the *Exatlón* camp,

I noticed one of the guards had left the keys in his bike. I saw a big keychain hanging and thought, *This fucking idiot left the key there. If I get on that bike, I'm gone.* I started chatting with the crew, then ran toward the bike. I got on and started trying to kick it into gear, but I kept stalling out in first gear. As I revved the engine and popped it into gear, I realized the bike had a faulty first gear. It was slipping, sputtering, and stalling out. The guards, realizing what was happening, started sprinting toward me, closing in from one hundred feet away. "Please, no!" they shouted. "Please, no!" I was desperately trying to start the fucking bike, not knowing I needed to shift to second gear. My whole team was shouting, "Go, go, go!" Finally, the guards got to me. "I wasn't trying to take off," I told them. "I was just messing with you."

They sent me back to my cabin. That's when I decided I was going to escape. I packed my bag, grabbed my machete, and headed for the jungle, ready to climb up one side of the mountain and descend on the other. I knew exactly where I'd end up, somewhere near a gas station. I spent three and a half hours chopping my way through the dense jungle. Finally I reached the bottom and saw I was near some farms. All of a sudden I see this big fucking humongous dog drinking water. *Oh, shit, I'm in somebody's spot,* I realized. I quietly backed away and found another path to avoid the property.

After a brief walk, I found myself on the edge of the road with the gas station a few hundred feet away. The Las Terrenas area of the Dominican Republic was where *Exatlón* and other reality TV shows were all filmed. If you went thirty minutes in any direction, you were bound to run into another show, whether it was *Survivor* or another *Exatlón* series. In those rural towns, everybody knew the stars on the shows; the city's economy was thriving and surviving off them. I couldn't cross the road unnoticed. If one of the buses or minivans saw me, I was fucked. I crouched down alongside the road behind a fence for thirty minutes—until I didn't see a steady stream of cars. I looked both ways, didn't see a car coming, leaped over the fence, and sprinted toward the gas station.

Right as I got to the parking lot, a guy pulled up and recognized me. "Masvidal! What are you doing out here?" he asked.

"I'm with Marisela," I responded, making up a story about me and the another contestant. "She's inside getting Gatorade. We're heading back that way to the nurse. I got hurt."

As I went inside the gas station, I saw him get on his walkie-talkie. *Shit.* I went inside to the bathroom, washed up quickly, and combed my hair. I came out acting casual and asked a guy gassing up his motorcycle for a ride toward the city.

"Mind if I catch a ride?" I asked. The guy was carrying a stack of propane tanks with him on this crazy fucking makeshift motorcycle but had just enough space to fit one more person.

We took off, flying through the mountains on the janky motorcycle. I was hanging on tight, one leg dangling off. I sat sideways, my leg locked in a propane tank and my arms holding on to the guy's shoulder. Despite the chaos, the ride was so peaceful. It was another reminder of how healing and rejuvenating my time in the nature was. After thirty minutes we got to the outskirts of town, where a bunch of locals who worked on the show lived. It didn't take long for one of them to recognize me.

"What are you doing here?" they asked.

"Bro, I escaped," I said. "I need your help."

I more or less had a plan figured out: I'd go to Puerto Rico, where my daughter didn't need a passport to visit from Miami. The Dominican Republic and Puerto Rico are close neighbors, and there were regular routes for immigrants traveling to the island. I'd see my daughter in Puerto Rico and then I'd come right back to the show. I just had to find someone to take me.

The guy took me into his house and gave me a change of clothes.

When we came out, the whole neighborhood knew I was there. The security crew from the show had arrived in the neighborhood looking for me. That's when the boy took me up the hill and the little old lady whisked me away and hid me under her bed. I laid there for two hours until I heard the knock.

THE END OF THE ROAD

"Jorge," Yousef said. "I know you're there."

Yousef was a Turkish security guard who I had gotten to know during my weeks on the show. I stayed under the bed, frozen, as he continued. "If you're listening, I'm gonna get fired when we get back. You know my situation back home. I just want to tell you that I know you're there and I'm sorry. If you don't come out, I won't even be mad at you. It's all good, brother."

Yousef's words fucking ate at me. He had nothing to do with my situation, but he knew the reason I was doing this. I crawled out from under the bed after hearing Yousef plead for me to come back. The lady fucking slapped me and yelled, "Get back under the bed!" But it was over; there was no escaping.

When I walked outside, the entire neighborhood had gathered and was going nuts. It was a small, poverty-stricken rural town and they were all excited. People were running up, handing me Styrofoam cups filled with alcohol. I started grabbing the cups and shooting them back. One of the top executives at Telemundo came up and asked me to get into the Suburban to talk. He'd come from an hour and a half away, so I knew it was serious. He was frustrated with my escape but knew I had been misled when I signed on to the show. The show aired on Telemundo, but my contract was with three Turkish guys who managed the production company. Despite the fact that Telemundo would be broadcasting the show, they weren't the ones making the rules. The two sides were battling for control of the show and I was caught in the middle. The Telemundo executive told me he'd do what he could so I could go see my daughter. I was skeptical but figured I'd go back to the *Exatlón* camp for the time being. What choice did I have?

That week our team was sent to a typical obstacle course for elimination. I was ready for when we'd go best of seven, but the other guy with the lowest score said he had a rib injury and couldn't compete. I figured I won by default.

Instead, they decided to settle it through a shooting competition. We were positioned on a staircase about ten feet high. The objective was to drop a ball onto the marble tiles below and see who broke the most. Back and forth it went, with me breaking two and then the other guy matching it. That's how they got me out. I was pissed. Running that course multiple times was my strength, and they knew it. The executives knew they couldn't control me and didn't want to see me in the finals. I'd collected a bunch of medals over the preceding weeks, which allowed me to take points away during competitions. I was saving them for the finals, but they didn't even give me a chance to use them. In the end, I was bitter about how it all played out, but I was ready to go home, back to my kids, and back to the Octagon.

TIME TO BAPTIZE PEOPLE

When I landed back in Miami after *Exatlón*, I couldn't wait to share my revelation with Dan, who had witnessed my highs and lows from the time I joined American Top Team more than a decade earlier. I called him when I got home.

"Hey, I need you to meet me," I told him.

CHAPTER 13

THE RESURRECTION

I missed fighting so fucking much. Not only was it all I knew, but it was all I ever liked to do. There were a million other ways I could have made a living, but let's be real: my favorite one by far was punching people in the face. And it felt like ages since I'd knocked a poor bastard out.

When I got back stateside in Miami, I hit the gym. My ass was in the best shape of my career, but it wasn't fighting shape. I needed to get back to work if I wanted to take on the top dogs in the welterweight division. I studied up on the rankings. Ranked dudes were lined up ahead of me, and I wanted to snatch everybody's head in the top ten and take their soul with it. When I looked at the other welterweights, I knew I had my work cut out for me, but every single one of these guys, I was going to baptize them. It was time to separate myself from the pack because, let's face it, my time was running out. My thirty-fourth birthday was a few weeks away. Shit, that was almost ancient for a fighter. I figured I had maybe three or four good years left in me to fight the best of the best in my division. I had to make them count. My sights were set on a title shot.

That winter there were talks about getting on the UFC 235 card the following spring against Nick Diaz. I wanted to fight the Diaz brothers—they were good jujitsu guys and great boxers, and they had that dog in them. I wanted to get in the cage with them and see who was more of a dog. But shit didn't materialize, and by the end of the year I was still without a fight. Back to the drawing board. I started calling fools out on Twitter. I tweeted at Neil Magny, the No. 10 guy: "I'm just waiting on a fight I need to get paid." I wanted to break his face. No dice.

As I eyeballed the welterweight rankings, there he was: third-ranked Darren Till, who seemed to be in the same situation. He was coming off his first loss to defending champion Tyron Woodley at UFC 228 a few months earlier, but the dude was 17-1-1. Till had it all: size, speed, power, and a left hand that could put your lights out. He'd fought for the title and got submitted, but it was on short notice. There had been rumors of Till moving up a division, but he decided to stick around at welterweight and couldn't find a fight. A lot of guys didn't want to fight Till because he had beat up on people. Everyone was still on the Darren Till hype train, but, fuck, I wasn't scared. He wasn't the best offensive grappler, so I didn't have to worry much about that. I knew if we fought, it was going to be a stand-up fight, and nobody was better on their feet than me.

I kept tabs on the UFC schedule and knew there was a London card coming up in eight weeks, but they'd announced only two fights. This was going to be in Till's hometown. I knew I could ride in on my white horse and steal the show and take the fucking wind out of everybody's sails. So, on the morning of January 14, 2019, I took my shot and called out Till on Twitter. "@darrentill2 I hear you having the same probs I am trying to find someone to fight you in your backyard. I love fighting in other peoples' backyards. I'm game if ufc can make it happen." Till tweeted back with a GIF of Jonah Hill, seemingly confirming his interest.

The UFC wasn't sure at first. Till was a young up-and-coming twenty-six-year-old who hadn't lost until a few months back. I'd just turned thirty-four a couple months earlier and hadn't stepped into the Octagon in damn near a year and a half. But I had some decent name recognition across the pond; I had already fought a couple of British guys. I beat Ultimate Fighter champ Ross Pearson and Paul Daley in the States. A few days after our Twitter back-and-forth, we had a deal to headline UFC Fight Night 147. Me and Till, the main event at the O2 in London.

I had this gut feeling that my resurrection was coming. In the Dominican Republic, I could finally hear my voice, and it wasn't drowned out by a million opinions or some dumbass song on the radio. Just my voice, contemplating what I wanted to achieve in my life before I closed the chapter on fighting. I reverse engineered all the shit—what went right, what went wrong—and crafted my new formula. No more dancing around, trying to outpoint a dude. It was time to end them, no judges involved. That was my game plan for the rest of my career. I was ready to come back. I wasn't finished. I had already spent sixteen years in the fight game, beating down a lot of good guys, but I hadn't broken through. I was always confident and cocky, but I put in the work. After months in the jungle, with this new mindset, I wasn't just confident; I was convinced. I was certain of my destiny.

I knew Till would come at me. From the interviews, the way he fought, opponents we had had in common, I knew it was going to be a fight. Going to England, I knew winning a decision wasn't in the cards for me, no matter what I did. I had to beat him by knockout or submission. England wasn't going to decide my fate. I needed to land there and drop the fucking bomb on this guy's face.

QUIET AS A MOTHERFUCKING PIN DROP

The UFC announced "UFC Fight Night: Till vs. Masvidal" as the main event for UFC 147 on January 16, exactly two months before our matchup. Till was ranked No. 3 and there I was, sitting at No. 11. It had been more than sixteen months since I stepped in the cage. People out there saw me as the stepping stone for Till to climb back to another title shot. But I had other plans.

Training camp was a motherfucker. I came in the best shape of my life after all that running and sprinting in the Dominican Republic. I had a nice hill where I could sprint, or I would run on the beach for long periods, four to six miles or until my legs stopped working. I couldn't track how long I had been running—they took all our possessions away—so I'd just run until I was fucking hurting. I mixed in shadowboxing in my room. That wasn't real training, but it got my body and mind right. Now, leading up to UFC 147, I had to get my body used to fighting again: wrestling, scrapping, throwing kicks—muscles I hadn't used in months.

It took a minute to get my wind back, but I got it all back. Jason David Frank, rest in peace, was a crucial part of my camp. He was a big guy, 185 pounds, and he'd go southpaw, helping me prepare for Till. We worked our asses off. Chris "Maluco" Thorne was another solid dude who got in the trenches with me. It took a bit to get those specific muscles firing right, but when they did, it was like fireworks going off. There was excitement all around. I was in killer shape, beating my sparring partners, dialed the fuck in. Everyone was excited about what was going to go down in London.

The week of the fight, I jacked my knee up in training camp. I was in the middle of a wrestling scrum and I banged it up real bad. Instead of complaining, I decided I'd make Till's knee hurt just as bad. I planned to sprint across the cage at him right off the bell and fucking kick him in the knee. On the day of the fight, as soon as we touched gloves, I went for it full speed. But at the last second he shifted sideways and I missed by inches, instead kicking him in the nuts. *Fuck!* I'd been out sixteen months and I committed a low blow right from the jump.

I didn't get a point taken away since it was incidental, but it wasn't exactly how I had planned my return.

Fifteen seconds after we restarted, Till closed in quick and dropped me with a beautiful straight left to the side of my face. I didn't see it coming. I wasn't even sure what the fuck he hit me with. I just knew I wanted to kill him. I sat on the mat, stuck out my tongue, and grinned. That was the moment. You could see the expression on my face. It was like a switch flipped in my head. That's when I knew, *This is where I belong, in the fucking fight world.* I didn't expect Till to drop me that night, but, hey, you have to expect the unexpected in fighting. He took me down twice in the first round, capitalizing again later in the round on a kick I threw. He was going hard, trying to finish me, but I hugged him after the second drop and remember telling myself, *If he doesn't finish me here, I'm gonna get his ass.* He was burning a lot of energy.

Between rounds, my corner was telling me the usual: Hands up, move your head, find your range. I already knew I was timing his moves better toward the end of the round. You get all this advice in sixty seconds between rounds: Breathe, relax, and sharpen your technique. My coaches see things I can't in the heat of the moment. I might be too amped up and wild, not fighting smart. Those moments provide little reminders to help when I'm flooded with adrenaline and can't think straight. For this fight, their advice was crucial. After almost a year and a half off, I needed to hear those small adjustments to get my head right. My coaches said to open up more in the next round. That's exactly what I planned to do.

After five minutes studying Till in the first round, I had a read on him—the length of his extremities, his footwork, his speed, his timing. I knew exactly what I could do to him. I started putting the game plan from the gym into action, using the techniques and footwork I'd drilled for this matchup. As soon as round two started, I opened up on his ass. I was countering everything he threw, pushing him back—and then I totally switched the momentum. Right away he knew it was a different match. He landed some good jabs, a couple of straight lefts, but nothing that shocked me. I controlled that round from the start.

With two minutes left in the second round, I switched to southpaw and threw a right jab to set up a huge left hook that crashed right on his jaw. That left hook put his ass out. The second the shot landed, Till's soul left his body. His eyes went blank and he toppled backward. I threw a couple more jabs on the way down to be sure. The medics rushed in to check him. It was fucking ugly. The hometown crowd went quiet. Silent as a motherfucking pin drop. That feeling right there, that's a drug like nothing else. I love the chants and the cheering, but sometimes that silence is the sweetest sound. I stood in the center of the cage, my hand raised in victory in enemy territory, the soul sucked out of the place. I had just taken a giant leap to where I belonged—on top.

"I need that belt wrapped around my waist," I shouted to the stunned crowd. "Dana White, get behind me. I might not have a whole country behind me but I have the whole world behind me."

THREE-PIECE WITH THE SODA

I was standing in front of the ESPN backdrop in the back of O2 Arena, fresh off putting Till's lights out, doing my post-fight interview with Laura Sanko, when I caught a glimpse of Leon Edwards strolling behind the camera guy.

Edwards and I didn't have any real history between us. He had called me out on Twitter before I went on *Exatlón*, and I shot back saying I'd fight him. Then I went to the Dominican Republic and nothing materialized. While I was gone, he was talking shit, saying I was ducking him. I didn't have any respect for him. I had knocked out guys that he went to decisions with; he wasn't shit. He needed to keep my name out of his mouth. He was on the card as a co-main and had been talking trash, saying he should have been the one fighting Till in the main event instead of me. After I knocked Till out, Edwards walked past the ESPN backdrop, about ten feet away. This time he wasn't hiding behind a keyboard or a phone screen.

"How about us next?" Edwards shouted. "July?"

I glanced toward Edwards and shrugged.

"Maybe, maybe not," I shouted back.

"Ah, shut up," he said.

He kept walking. *Not today, motherfucker*, I thought.

"Hey," I said, "come over here and say it to my face, bro."

I started walking away from the interview toward him, hands behind my back to signal I wasn't there for trouble. When I got close, he put his hands up and came toward me aggressively. Where I come from, when someone puts their hands up like that, it means only one thing: they're about to throw down. We squared up across the metal rail. *Boom!* I unleashed a quick combo to his face before security yanked us apart. I had caught him right across the left eye, cutting it open. I'm not saying it was the ideal way to handle business, but when someone is disrespecting you, you gotta do what you gotta do to defend yourself.

As the chaos unfolded, the video of our skirmish went viral, racking up over 6 million views. "Let's get the fuck out of here," I told my manager, Abe. But Abe knew better. "It's better if we tell our side of the story," he told me. The world was already forming its narrative, thinking I just walked up and attacked this guy unprovoked. That wasn't how it went down. So we agreed to an interview with ESPN. Brett Okamoto came back into the locker room and I sat down to explain myself.

I told him what happened: that this hooligan Edwards had been talking crap on social media, I saw him there, and he didn't address me as a man. I was in England and didn't want to incriminate myself by admitting I punched him. So I just said some slang from back home. "You're not gonna get a hit off me," I said. "So I give him the three-piece with the soda, and then just glide outta there." I didn't think much of it at the time, just speaking my truth. But that shit became a catchphrase overnight. Growing up, we'd always joke like that after someone got clocked: "Ah, you got hit with a three-piece and a biscuit" or "Three-piece and a soda." It just came to mind and ended up blowing up. The YouTube videos got millions of views, and people started making T-shirts and merch with the saying.

After the interview, I left for Turkey and had a great time. I'm a thug from the streets; I didn't care what the fuck the UFC was going to do. Edwards started it by disrespecting me during my interview. You're going to tell me to shut up while I'm talking? That was the UFC's fault for not having security there to protect us, and I thought Dana White agreed. They knew how I operated. If somebody disrespects me, I don't mind fighting. I'm not going to go tattle. No, I'll handle it myself. That's how I've always been my whole life.

All that was on my mind was what was next. I knew the recipe for success: Minimize distractions and stay focused on training for the next fight. Don't get caught up in the allures of fame and money and life. Just keep my head down and focus on the next opponent. I was already back in the gym before my next fight was announced, getting a head start on whoever the UFC gave me.

I started taking off after my fight in London. People called it the Resurrection, and it fucking was. It was like I came back from the dead. Every fight in my career led to the next. I was an OG in the sport. I had come from fighting backyard fights for Kimbo fucking Slice; I was as real as it gets. What you see is what you get with me, no bullshit. That's what people liked. When you combine that with me putting everything together, my career was ready to explode. People wanted to embrace me because I was fucking real, and my journey was crazy.

For so long, my career had been marked by a lot of close calls and disappointment. You don't see many fighters emerge in their mid-thirties after forty-five fucking pro bouts and a year and a half away from the sport. The odds of that happening are near zero. But it happened to me. I knew this was just the start. The best was yet to come.

CHAPTER 14

FIVE SECONDS

Before I flatlined Till in London, a loudmouth named Ben Askren was already maneuvering for the next fight. The dude had won one UFC fight in his life and thought he was hot shit. When I got to London, nobody gave me a chance against the hometown hero Till. I was a nearly 2-to-1 underdog. Everyone figured Till would beat me and then he'd fight Askren next. Guess no one told me the plan, because I knocked Till's ass straight out.

Askren flew to London trying to set up a fight. The UFC even gave him his own press conference. "I'm here to pick a fight with Darren Till or Jorge Masvidal," he announced. The dude was a fucking groupie. He was always making wisecracks on Twitter. He was particularly obsessed with Till, always trying to gear up for a fight. He thought Till was going to beat me and he'd finally get what he wanted. "I want Darren Till," he told the crowd. "He's right back there." Till walked out from behind the curtain, flipping birds, yelling "Fuck Ben Askren!" Askren was a former Bellator champ who was 19-0 in MMA after beating Robbie Lawler in his UFC debut. Lawler almost decapitated him on a slam in the fight, busted up his face, and then referee

Herb Dean bailed him out and he won on a controversial sub. He pranced over Lawler's body. What a little bitch. There was talk of an Askren-versus-Lawler rematch but Askren wasn't interested. After I knocked Till to the canvas, Askren shifted his focus to me. "Kind of sad about Till, that was gonna be fun," he tweeted. Then he followed it up after my backstage clash with Edwards, "Masvidal just started a fight backstage with Leon Edwards so he doesn't have to fight me next." The dude was a keyboard warrior.

During negotiations with the UFC after the Till fight, it was either Edwards or Askren, and Askren was much higher ranked. So I took it. Something happened during camp, and the UFC wanted to pull Askren for a different fight, maybe a rematch with Lawler. But the contract was signed, and I'd already been training for him for six weeks. "Fuck no," I said. It was tempting to take a striker like Edwards, but I was too far down the road prepping for Askren. "Nah, you know what? I've been training for Ben," I said. "It's fucking Ben. Leave it like that."

I got back from Turkey after celebrating the Till win and hit the gym immediately. I had a full twelve weeks to prepare for Askren, so my gas tank was way ahead of the curve. I had one thought driving me each session: *I'm gonna kill somebody.*

Askren was always popping off on social media or talking shit in the media. It was like he spent all day googling shit and looking up jokes on Twitter. That wasn't me. I didn't live on Twitter. From a distance, social media arguments just look like two fools. I wasn't interested in arguing with fools online. Here and there I'd fire back, but I liked to handle shit face-to-face. I mostly stayed off Twitter in camp and didn't give many interviews. Askren could talk all he wanted. My manager would email me Askren's tweets every once in a while to fire me up and my friends sometimes pulled out their phones to show me some shit he'd posted online or told the media. "I think it's pretty easy," Askren said in one interview. "He's simple, right? He's got good hands but his wrestling's not great. His jujitsu's not great. His strength is not great. His cardio is not great. So when you break it down like that, it becomes pretty simple."

Sweet, I thought, *I'ma kick his ass regardless.* All that did was confirm what I thought: the dude was a bitch. Askren wasn't my chick. I wasn't going to waste time messaging back and forth on Twitter. Every time I saw him face-to-face or at a press conference, I shut him down. That's what mattered to me. In Las Vegas at the weigh-in, Askren arrived with another one of his corny, calculated lines.

"Why are you so mad?" he asked, laughing.

I just smiled. I wasn't going to play his game. I didn't think anything of him; I just didn't like the dude. My goal was simple: make sure his bloodline didn't reproduce. As I said in an interview, it was the extinction of the Askren blood by the Masvidal blood. Beating him wasn't enough. I wanted to destroy his legs so he couldn't walk. I wanted him to say, *That fucking Masvidal, bro.* It was game over for that little punk. I just wanted to fuck him up.

A few days before the fight, I was walking around at the MGM Grand when a fan handed me a drawing. It was me stepping on Askren's face. They wanted me to fuck up his face. I was happy to oblige.

THE FLYING KNEE

Months after my loss to Paul Rodriguez in 2005, that flying knee still haunted my dreams. I threw the knee trying to hurt him, but it was flawed from the start. My technique had been trash—the infrastructure, everything. When he backed up, I missed and he dropped me, took my back, and got the choke. It took time to regroup after that loss. But I started investing time to learn the knee, drilling that knee

165

nonstop to make it my own. It had been nearly fourteen years of practice leading into UFC 239.

Once the Askren fight got booked, I thought, *I'm going to beat this guy's ass for fifteen minutes.* I knew Askren could wrestle and that was it. After a few weeks of studying him closer, I decided, *You know what? I'm going to check him right out the gate and see where he's at.* I knew that changing speeds on him and making him uncomfortable would force him into his natural instincts—which was crotch sniffing. I thought if I changed speed and blasted him from the start, he was going to level change and shoot for the legs. I had a good feeling that if he ducked, he was going to die. I told Coach Brown of the plan a few weeks into training. We practiced it relentlessly in camp, incorporating the knee into sparring sessions; we must have practiced it a hundred times. It wasn't easy to train for, either, mostly because I didn't want to kill my training partners.

A lot of fighting is psychological: getting in your opponent's head to understand the way they think. I always studied my opponents closely, in the cage and outside it. I watched how they carried themselves, trying to understand their mindset. On Twitter, I saw Askren was pretty witty, constantly cracking jokes. He was a dork but quick on the keyboard. But when I saw him in person, I saw how weak he was. Anytime we saw each other face-to-face, when it was unscripted, my improvisation versus his, he'd freeze up. I saw him in the hotel lobby before the fight and popped out as he walked by. He short-circuited. "What's up, boss?" he muttered, avoiding eye contact. I noticed every unplanned interaction, when it was spur-of-the-moment, he couldn't fucking keep it together. On the fly, he had nothing. The dude couldn't improvise for shit.

The night before the fight, I was 95 percent sure the plan would work. All I had to do was make him uncomfortable and his instincts would take over. I visualized the knee landing over and over, like a basketball player practicing the game-winning shot. That opening knee sequence was just one of endless scenarios that could happen. It's a fight: I had to prepare plans and backups for anything that could happen. I visualized five counter-solutions for every possible path. If he shot for a takedown, I'd stuff it and deliver the knee. But what would happen if he took me down? I had to be ready to slip out and reverse. What if he caught me in his choke? How did I plan to get out? The flying knee was just one option. And even if the knee worked, it didn't mean the fight would be over. I pictured the knee landing on his shoulder as he ducked it, injuring him but not finishing him. My visualizations were like a Navy SEAL prepping for a mission, running through every angle of attack and defense. Contingencies on contingencies. I was mentally rehearsing every sequence, seeing all the ways the fight could unfold. When it was time, I'd flow wherever it went.

On fight day Coach Brown and I drilled the knee up until the very end to make sure my footwork and timing were right. I just had to enter his space and he would do the rest. If I just changed the speed on him, he was going to fucking duck. I knew it. I had to take advantage. Right before the fight, I stared at Askren from across the cage. "You gotta come prove it now," I told him.

I was ready. I was letting that knee fly regardless. If he ducked, he was going to fucking die. If not, I'd still hit him and keep the fight going. My mind was empty. I knew what I had to do. I just had to go execute what I'd practiced for weeks.

I came out slow and cut the angle to bait him. As soon as I changed speeds, what did he do? He went to his instincts and dropped levels, just like I knew he would. I threw the knee and he went low. *Bang!* More or less, it was over in three seconds; they called it at five but he went stiff before. I landed two more shots until the ref pulled me off. Some people were pissed, but it was necessary. My job was to hit somebody until the ref pulled me off. I didn't understand why some people were upset. He was allowed to do and say whatever he wanted, talking wild about my manhood, my culture, my ethnicity, even my kids, but I couldn't showboat? It was just business.

I'd visualized the knee thousands of times, but when it happened for real, it felt surreal. At the same time, it wasn't surprising: I'd already seen it play out in my head. It felt quick, and I wondered if I had broken a record. Sure enough, the announcer confirmed it: the fastest KO ever at five seconds. Duane Ludwig had held the record for more than thirteen years at six seconds. Now the UFC record was mine. We all celebrated in the locker room afterward. A bunch of fighters from the card came by to congratulate me on the record. Dana White called it one of the most vicious knockouts he'd ever witnessed.

It took sixteen years to get to that moment and then just five seconds to completely alter the trajectory of my career. At the time, I wasn't the highest-paid fighter. I was known to hard-core MMA fans but not a household name. That KO changed all of that. I instantly had more negotiation leverage and tripled my salary. Then it exponentially increased with each fight. My social media following doubled from 350,000 to 750,000 almost overnight. It was madness. It just kept climbing and climbing. That moment is *the* timestamp in my life.

You don't see meteoric rises overnight—and, truthfully, mine took years of blood, sweat, and tears behind the scenes to have that night in the Octagon. All the grueling hours of preparation set the stage for my arrival, but five seconds turned me from underdog to the hottest fucking name in MMA.

CHAPTER 15

BMF

I wasn't sure what was next after the viral five-second knockout. Six weeks had passed since I iced Askren, and I was back grinding in the gym, staying sharp just in case. I wanted a third marquee matchup to cap the year, but there were no signs of a title shot coming from negotiations with the UFC. So I headed to UFC 241 in Anaheim to watch the fights. I never expected I'd leave with my next fight teed up.

I was sitting cageside, watching Nate Diaz dominate Anthony Pettis in the main event, his first fight back in three years. I always respected Diaz's game. He had burst onto the UFC scene with a victory over Conor McGregor in 2016. And with his unanimous decision against Pettis that night he was about to debut back in the top ten. I was watching as a fan when out of nowhere in his post-fight interview with Joe Rogan, Diaz called me out. "The reason I was off is because everybody sucked, and there was nobody to fight. But with this belt, I want to defend it against . . . Jorge Masvidal," Diaz said. "Had a good last fight. All respect to the man, but there ain't no gangsters in this game anymore. There ain't nobody who's done it right but me and him. I know my man's a gangster, but he ain't no West Coast gangster."

I raised my fist to pump up the crowd. *Hell yeah*, I thought, *this guy is calling me out.* After the Askren knockout, a lot of top guys didn't want to fight me. But Diaz was giving me a chance to take out another big name in the same year. The last time somebody had finished three top-five opponents in one calendar year had been Matt Hughes. Sure, everybody fights three times a year, but not everyone takes on top-five guys. It would be a big fucking accomplishment for me to pull it off.

Diaz called himself the Baddest Motherfucker and said I was the runner-up. There was only one way to determine the true BMF. Fans wanted that fight badly. The anticipation took on a life of its own, fueled by the fans and the media, but for a few weeks the UFC wasn't taking the fight seriously. Diaz had called me out, but talks circled around a 2020 date. The UFC initially was trying to book Kamaru Usman versus Colby Covington in a title fight at Madison Square Garden, but the deal fell apart due to Colby's demands. They checked with my team. I was ready, but the UFC couldn't get Usman to agree. Edwards was considered, but those talks hit a wall too. With nothing else lining up for MSG in November, it became a golden opportunity. The stars aligned, and in less than a day a deal was sealed. Diaz versus Masvidal. New York City. Madison Square Garden. Pay-per-view. All to decide the Baddest Motherfucker.

When we put the deal together, nobody knew about a possible BMF belt. That was an unexpected bonus from Dana White. He decided a belt should be in play, and the UFC spent fifty grand to craft the Baddest Motherfucker belt. Dwayne "the Rock" Johnson agreed to put the BMF belt around the winner. It was cool as hell, and it made sense. The Baddest Motherfucker—I claimed the label, as did peers in my sport. Diaz believed he was. So why not put it to the test?

The fight had been scheduled for nearly two months when a tweet came across my feed just nine days before the fight. I couldn't believe my eyes. *What the fuck? It has to be Photoshopped.* I dug a little harder. Nope, that shit was real. Diaz tweeted that he had tested positive for a banned substance. The fight was off. My mind was racing. I knew Diaz wasn't a cheater. I figured he had too much CBD or something. *Would they really cancel the fight?* The anxiety hit hard. Whenever that dark cloud comes, I start to unravel. I immediately sunk into depression. I picked up my phone, went to Uber Eats, and started ordering. Two pizzas, hot fries, and several bottles of Mexican soda later, I was on the couch, stuffed. I fucked up a lot of food. Papa Dukes lived with me and called in the cavalry. My coaches showed up and calmed my anxiety down. They took the credit cards and saved me from myself. A day later, the UFC cleared Diaz: the positive test had just been tainted multivitamins. Fight on.

This was a legacy fight. Not because it was at MSG, not because of the BMF belt, and not because it was the five hundredth card in UFC history. It was about Diaz. Whether we fought in a parking lot or in his backyard, it was destined to be a big fight. Diaz was a dog and I was a dog. We were both savage fighters who brought it every time. I always wanted to fight the best of the best. It was a dream matchup, complete with the title of "Baddest Motherfucker" and a shiny belt for the winner.

I had major respect for Diaz, but I was going to New York to do one thing: damage. The only way to separate myself from the pack was to send Diaz to another dimension.

ON TOP OF THE WORLD

Going into camp for Diaz, I was already in peak shape. My last camp for Askren had been a grueling twelve weeks. I pushed myself to the limit every day, thirty-minute sessions drilling that flying knee over and over. UFC fights don't last long, but I was revved up and wanted to have a ton of gas left in the tank when the call came.

But my right hand was a fucking mess. I didn't have any injuries from the Askren fight; it had taken only five seconds. It was camp that brutalized my hands. When they first mentioned the Diaz fight would be in 2020, I thought, *Whatever.* My hand was destroyed and I could use the time to heal up. But the UFC tossed the BMF title into the mix, and I couldn't say no to a third headline fight in a year. I figured I'd deal with the pain after I got the job done. Going into the Diaz fight, that hand was still destroyed. Ligaments, tendons, the whole thing. At the beginning of camp, I wasn't even throwing it, but as camp rolled on, I had to see if I could use the hand or not. It hurt like hell but I sucked it up, put on the pads, and got through camp. We studied Diaz and came up with a killer game plan. It was all about breaking Diaz down with kicks, owning the clinch, and then beating him up in the clinch. If the fight hit the mat, I had to be the one on top, controlling the pace. It was simple but deadly.

When fight week arrived, I got word that President Donald Trump was going to be at MSG for my scrap with Diaz—the first sitting president ever to attend a UFC event. I was fucking humbled but I had to stay focused on the task at hand. The night of the fight, trying to get to MSG was madness with all the extra security and Secret Service closing down the city for Trump's arrival. Manhattan was practically shut down, all the streets closed around the arena. My hotel was half a mile away, and it took over an hour just to reach MSG. My team wouldn't let me get out and walk because they were worried about me getting mugged because there were so many people going to the fight. So we slowly drove the ten blocks to the arena.

The atmosphere was already buzzing when the card got underway. Throw in the Rock's presence—he was there because he was going to wrap the BMF belt around the winner, after all—and it was mayhem.

Around 10 p.m. President Trump walked onto the floor right before the main event. It was pure fucking pandemonium. Having the leader of the free world choose my fight as the first UFC event to attend was fucking bananas. Walking to the cage, I glanced over and saw Trump sitting cageside. I knew all eyes were on me. The atmosphere was nuts and I soaked it in, but as soon as that cage door shut, it was time to focus on the reason I was there. Stepping across from Diaz, Trump, and 20,000 fans faded into the background. I was laser focused on one thing that night: proving once and for all who the Baddest Motherfucker truly was.

I decided to mess with Diaz a bit to open the fight, pretending to throw the same flying knee that I used on Askren. It got a smile and it was game on. We clinched up early, just like I'd planned during camp, and I broke off and unleashed a flurry, catching him with an elbow and a head kick. The move opened up a nasty gash over his eye, and Diaz dropped to the mat. He was hurt, but he's a competitor like me. He won't stay down; you have to practically kill him to beat him. Diaz came out swinging in the second round, trying to even it up, but I stayed composed and kept tagging him with combos. He kept wiping blood from his eyes as it poured down his face. I landed a huge right hand that wobbled him. I knew the clinch was his move, but not tonight; I kept cracking him with shots anytime we tied up. He snagged my ankle for a submission at the end of the second, but I slipped out as the round ended. My pace and pressure kept mounting in the third, and the gash above his eye widened. Between the third and fourth rounds, the doctor took a look at his eye and called the fight off. I was shocked—I hadn't expected to win that way—but I had delivered a beating.

It was a bittersweet way to win, getting my hand raised but not getting the chance to finish Diaz off. I had had visions of baptizing him for five rounds. But at the end of the day, my goal had been to do damage and leave no doubt. The crowd booed, and Diaz and his camp complained, but there was nothing weird about it. I had dropped Diaz three times and he had three cuts on his face by the time the doctor stopped the fight. Part of me was thinking, *I beat the dog shit out of you*, but the other part of me was, like, *I would have beat him even worse if the ref had never stepped in*. Diaz should have been thanking the ref for saving his life, not whining and saying he would have won in five rounds. He never hurt me, never even rocked me. He was just a walking punching bag. I didn't take kindly to those comments. I won all three rounds easily. The dude needed twenty-five stitches to sew up his face.

I didn't escape cleanly either. After the fight, both my hands were destroyed. One of my blows struck the top of Diaz's head with such shitty technique that my hand folded. My right hand was so fucked-up, I couldn't even bend it to wipe my ass. But you know what? It was worth every punch. The BMF belt was mine without question.

I didn't get to talk to President Trump, but he gave me a shout-out on Twitter after he left MSG: "Great fight Champ!"

What a fucking year.

Till. Askren. Diaz.

It felt fucking good. Twenty-nineteen was the year I'd been grinding toward my whole career, the breakthrough I knew would come eventually if I just stayed the course. Sixteen years deep, there was no longer any doubt: Jorge Masvidal had arrived. Fighter of the Year, Knockout of the Year—the accolades poured in, validating it all. I took over the fight game just like I had planned. It was no accident. It was the result of years of grinding, staying in the fucking gym, and doing what I'd done since I was a kid. I had had a plan, a formula for success, and I executed it. Years of 5 a.m. bike rides to the gym in the dark. Sleeping in my Pontiac so I could be right back in the gym the next morning. Countless rounds sparring until I could taste blood. Sacrificing relationships and chunks of my personal life. The lonely road when no one believed. All those setbacks and close calls. It was all worth it for that moment on top of the mountain.

My long journey is proof that you can chase your dream until the timing is right. Put in the work in obscurity and stay ready so you don't have to get ready. Execute the plan even when no one else sees your vision. Then one day the door opens. And when it swings open, it ain't the end of the fight; it's just a new round. The grind doesn't stop. The BMF title wasn't a destination; it was a badge earned every damn day.

People could debate my legacy and place in history. But in 2019, on the biggest stages, I proved to the world what I always knew: I was the Baddest Motherfucker.

CHAPTER 16

OPPORTUNITY KNOCKS

I wasn't sure what was next after I punched my way through 2019, but in my mind I was next in line to fight Kamaru Usman for the welterweight title. Me, Tyron Woodley, Colby Covington, Gilbert Burns, Leon Edwards, and Conor McGregor were all at the top of the crowded division, but after the way I baptized Till, Askren, and Diaz, there was no doubt that I should be the one to challenge Usman and take that belt from him. I had my sights set on that welterweight title, and after the resurrection I pulled off in 2019, I knew it was my turn.

Usman had claimed the welterweight belt in early 2019 with a unanimous decision against Woodley and then defended it by knocking out Covington at the end of the year. "The Nigerian Nightmare" was 11-0 in the UFC and his one and only MMA loss was his second professional fight, in 2013. It was my turn to take a shot at him. "He's the best out of each and every one of them," Usman said. "He's the next guy in front of me."

But then the coronavirus came along and fucked everything up. The UFC canceled all its events in March 2020 because of the pandemic. At first I thought they might shut down completely, which would've been a disaster for me. I was thirty-five and running out of time to win a championship. I couldn't lose another year. I needed to keep fighting.

For most sports leagues, COVID meant shutting down for God knows how long. But since UFC events only need two fighters and a ref, White saw an opportunity to keep going while other sports couldn't. Thank God that I was in the greatest country in the world, the United States, and in the best state in the country, Florida. Our governor, Ron DeSantis, made sure businesses could keep operating. He fought against restrictive policies, helping businesses like the UFC continue to schedule events when many states were shutting down. While travel restrictions and testing protocols remained a pain in the ass, DeSantis enabled Florida to reopen faster and set an example for the nation and world. It made a huge difference for me personally, letting me pursue that title I had my eyes on through the pandemic madness.

After six weeks of canceled events, the UFC started holding fights again in empty arenas in Florida and Vegas. Fans started coming back slowly. Attendance was capped at 30 percent capacity for a while, but thanks to DeSantis we bounced back faster than anywhere else. The United States was locked down, so if you weren't in America, you were screwed. But DeSantis's approach gave us with more freedom and liberty in Florida than we saw in lockdown states. As I've said before, he's the greatest governor of all time.

When White announced early in the pandemic that he had access to a private island that he could make available for UFC fights, it sounded like something out of a video game, like *Mortal Kombat* meets UFC or some shit. I knew all about Shang Tsung's Island from playing that game. But this so-called Fight Island wasn't just some crazy gimmick; it was nearly ten-square-mile Yas Island in Abu Dhabi. This man-made island had amusement parks, golf courses, resorts, and nice-ass beaches. And it allowed international fighters who couldn't enter the U.S. to compete. It wasn't a vacation—fighters would be confined to the bubble and could hardly leave the hotel—but it beat the shit out of sitting around at home, doing nothing. The UFC turned the tourist attraction into a private fighting facility and planned the first pay-per-view fight on the island for July 11.

I negotiated with the UFC all through the spring to book a title fight with Usman, but they lowballed me on the pay-per-view cut. I wasn't asking for more guaranteed money up-front. I just wanted a bigger percentage of the extra PPV sales I'd be generating. If me and Usman were the selling points of PPV, I felt we should get a cut. At that time, UFC fighters got maybe 12 percent of the PPV revenue at most, but if I brought in more money, I wanted a bigger cut. That's the most—most—anybody ever got, and that was considered *Holy fuck, you got that much money?* Usually, guys were getting 8 percent. I felt like the UFC was trying to give me a raw deal. When I fought in Strikeforce for the belt, I hardly made any money. After a seven-week training camp, because they kept pushing that fight back, I got maybe $14,000 but I still had to pay my coaches. *What the fuck am I doing? What did I make here?* I always told myself, *The next time I fight for a world title, I'm gonna make sure I get paid.* When I fought for the BMF title against Diaz, I got paid a little something, but this fight I was talking about with the UFC was for the *world title.* I wanted to make sure I got paid what I was worth. I already knew about how the PPV percentages and payouts worked from the first time I fought Diaz. I hadn't liked that deal at the time and now I felt that the UFC was doing me dirty: they were offering me *less* for a bigger fight. The UFC offered me half of what I got for the Diaz fight, even though a title match with Usman would sell more PPV packages.

I went back and forth with the UFC negotiating for weeks

without getting anywhere. I put a deal on the table, but the UFC claimed the budget wasn't there. The price tag that I put out there they didn't wanna pay. "I'm not gonna do this," I told the UFC. Things were falling apart, so I took matters into my own hands. On June 5, I picked up my phone and went to Twitter. It caused a shit-storm.

If I'm not worth it let me go.

Why make me fight for half of what I made on my last fight 'cause the other dude can't draw?

History lesson for all the new fans that might have just started following my beautiful sport: 16 years been at this. Never once turned down a fight. Asked to go fight #3 at the time in his hometown across the pond after a year off. KO of the year nominee. Asked to fight #5 at the time and let's be real didn't have to fight him. Fast-est KO in the history of UFC. MSG I am asked to fight 3 different guys and I said yes to all three. I fought in backyards and those dudes never disrespected me the way I'm being now.

They told me he asked for way too much. They playing us.

It struck a nerve. White held a press conference later that day and addressed my firestorm with the media: "I think everybody wants more money. I think everybody wants more money in all these other sports. Masvidal says, 'You've got enough money to buy islands.' Let me repeat for the fucking billionth time: I did not buy an island, okay? We did not buy an island."

I fired back.

> Please don't compare us to these other leagues. I wish
> we can negotiate for less pay like the other leagues where
> the players get half the revenue they generate. We are
> negotiating from like what 12% to maybe 18% of revenue
> we generate? We are negotiating down from way under
> 50% of the revenue. I don't get paid on the hot dog you
> sell in the arena or the logo on the cage. I've never made
> a dollar on a ticket you sell. I get punched in the face for a
> living and even I know the pandemic or what's left of it has
> nothing to do with it. I'm not an independent contractor if
> I can't go anywhere else to make a living. Let me go and
> let me see if I'm worth it.

There were more talks between the UFC and my manager, but the
UFC didn't budge. I sent off a few more tweets on June 7.

> The negotiation is take it or leave it. If I lose you can cut
> me and not pay out the rest of the contract. If I win I'm
> not in a position to renegotiate the contract? My dad left
> a communist regime and has prepared me my whole
> life. Why are all the major names having issues? Conor,
> Jones, Cejudo. We have to take it or retire. I love fighting
> and this is the fight of our lives.

After two months, the negotiations were all but over. The UFC
made a final offer, but I wasn't satisfied. No title fight. On June 9, the
UFC announced "UFC 251: Usman vs. Gilbert Burns," their big PPV
debut on Fight Island.

Lots of fighters said I was a fucking idiot to turn down a title shot.
And a lot of fighters were, like, *Damn right, get yours.* I didn't care what
people thought. I can be a team player, but this was about taking a
stand for myself and my family. The fighters that saw eye to eye with

me—this was for them too. And if they didn't see eye to eye with me, fuck, this was still for them. We deserved to get paid based on the revenue we generated, not whatever crumbs the promoters wanted to throw us. I hoped I could make more money so the next guy could make more money and then the next guy and the guy after that. That's how it works in every other major sport, so why wouldn't the UFC be the same?

After negotiations with the UFC fell apart, I had no idea what was next. I didn't know when my next fight would come or if things would ever smooth over after that Twitter beef with the UFC. But then, just a week before UFC 251 on Fight Island, Burns tested positive for COVID.

I was home in Miami and about to dig into a box of cookies I had just ordered from Midnight Cookies & Cream when I saw the news. *Holy smokes! Is this true?* It was almost midnight, but I made some calls to confirm it was legit. Sure as shit, it was. I decided I wasn't going to eat one cookie until I got closure. Something told me not to eat. The next day I went to my manager Abe's July 4 backyard barbecue. He had resumed some negotiations with the UFC but they weren't budging and were still playing hardball. I asked him what the chances were that I'd get the Usman fight. "No shot," he told me. But Abe knew how badly I wanted it, so he called Hunter Campbell, an executive vice president at the UFC. They went back and forth for hours with no progress. I was getting tired. I issued an ultimatum. "Well, I've already fasted for twenty-four hours. It'll be twenty-six in no time," I said. "You guys need to tell me 'yes' or 'no,' but in an hour I'm going to start eating and then I'm not cutting any more weight." I was ready to start eating and giving up on making weight. They called back ten minutes later and gave me everything I had asked for. They should have paid me in the first place, but now I had them by the balls since it was last minute.

We had a deal: me versus Usman for the title on Fight Island. The only catch? I had six days instead of a full eight-week camp to cut weight and get ready. When the UFC agreed to my demands, I was smoking a fucking backwood: tobacco with marijuana. I took one last puff, stopped smoking, and got straight to the gym to start cutting. I was 190 pounds, with twenty left to go before weigh-ins in less than a week. It was going to be hell, but I was willing to walk through fire to get that belt. The UFC didn't wanna pay me before, but I was willing to bet on myself.

THE TWILIGHT ZONE

I got in a quick workout on July 5 to continue my weight cut before we jetted to Las Vegas from Miami. I had to pass a COVID test in Miami to get cleared for the flight. When we landed in Vegas, it would be time for another test. If mine came back negative, I'd finally get to head to Abu Dhabi and get to fight, assuming I didn't test positive for COVID.

At that time Coach Brown had been staying at my house. We did fucking everything together: eating, training, chilling. On the way to the airport, we were crammed into a car together for several hours. When we got to Vegas and took COVID tests, guess what happened? Even though I had just tested negative in Miami, Coach Brown tested positive and couldn't travel. There went my cornerman. I continued to test negative, but the whole situation was like stepping on pins and needles.

Once I was cleared, we boarded a private flight to begin the fourteen-hour trip from Vegas to Abu Dhabi. The whole world was coping with the coronavirus, so everything about the situation was bizarre. We couldn't even get off the plane when we stopped to refuel because of COVID restrictions. I was starving, and we managed to sneak some pizzas on board when we stopped in Italy. I took one bite of a pizza and spit out half of it. *I shouldn't have even fucking bit that thing*, I thought. I felt guilty, like I shouldn't be eating because I was trying to cut weight.

We landed in Abu Dhabi and there were immediately people in hazmat suits shoving swabs up my nose—more fucking testing. It was like I had walked into the epicenter of an outbreak. Every day they came to my hotel room to swab my nose and test me again. I still had to cut fifteen more pounds in less than a week before the fight. On top of that, Eastern Time in the U.S. was eight hours behind, and the UFC wanted the main event at 6 a.m. local time so it would be prime time back home. *This is nuts but I signed up for it*, I told myself. The UFC put us up in a nice-ass hotel on Yas Island, like a paradise in the desert. But don't get it twisted: we were quarantined in a bubble. No sightseeing or beach time, just a fight camp in a hotel. "Fight Hotel," my American Top Team teammate Daniel Poirier called it, and damn if he wasn't spot-on. It wasn't no tropical paradise with crashing waves and beach parties. Sitting in that hotel room, cutting weight, was a whole different beast, a mental prison more than an escape.

After a few days locked in my room, the walls started closing in on me mentally. They wouldn't let you step outside, not even for a breath of fresh air. Just staring at the same four walls, hour after hour, it messes with your mind. Makes you feel like you've slipped into some different version of reality. One day I was looking at my phone at the news back home and it only made it seem more bizarre. Kanye West was running for president. *What the fuck is going on?* It felt like the Twilight Zone. I needed some air bad, so I left my room and headed to the lobby. Five hotel security guys swarmed me immediately. "Can you please go back in your room, Mr. Masvidal? I'm so sorry to bother you," they said. "We can't have any guests walking in the lobby." *Fucking-A, bro*, I thought. It didn't feel like reality. I was used to cutting weight in saunas, and now I was surviving in a bubble. It was a mental game as much as it was physical. It didn't feel like it was real, but I knew what I was fucking there for and it was a fucking fight. That's the only thing I knew was real.

I was preparing on the fly for Usman, but I knew what I had to do: get in his face, avoid takedowns, and fight with everything I had. It was going to be uphill because I wasn't in peak shape and Usman was good at neutralizing guys like me. He doesn't stand and bang; he takes guys down and lays on them, stalling for rounds. But I was 100 percent committed to beating him and taking that title belt. After all the crazy shit leading up to the event, it finally felt like things were coming together. That week EA Sports announced to the world that I'd be on the cover of *EA Sports UFC 4,* along with Israel Adesanya. After my rocket rise in 2019, they wanted me front and center. I went from being a downloadable character in the game to being on the cover. Talk about Twilight Zone: I started out grinding in backyards, and now I was featured as one of the UFC's biggest stars. It confirmed that I must be doing something right. The formula that I came up with back in those jungles was paying dividends.

Walking into the empty Flash Forum on Fight Island was eerie. There were no fans, just some staff, producers, and a few VIPs. The seats were mostly empty, but it felt like the entire MMA world was watching. In just one week the fight sold a monster 1.3 million PPV packages, one of the biggest numbers ever for the UFC. It was only the sixth time the UFC had ever reached that PPV number out of hundreds of events. That meant the UFC was making something like $80 million. That's what my entire demands had been about from the start of negotiations. After all my battles just to get here, it was humbling to see how far I'd come. All eyes were on Fight Island.

I came into Fight Island with the odds stacked against me: short notice, minimal preparation, and facing a dominant opponent like

Usman. But I've never been one to back down from a challenge. I came out aggressive, pushing the pace with right combinations and hard kicks to Usman's legs and body. Knowing the challenges of stepping in on short notice, I wanted to finish things early if I could get a shot in. His game plan was to wear me out, and late in the first round he caught me with a leg kick that shifted the fight to the mat—exactly where he wanted it. I started to get gassed after round one. Usman weathered the storm and slowed me down, grinding me against the fence and scoring takedowns from the second round on. My wrestling looked good fending off his takedowns, but I made mistakes and my gas tank was running low. As the fight went on, I fell into a deeper hole that I couldn't climb out of. By round four I was exhausted and couldn't fire off punches and kicks to stop his pressure. I got to my feet in the closing seconds and threw off a flying knee and hard kicks trying to get the KO, but it was too little, too late. I had lost a unanimous decision.

People were impressed that I had survived twenty-five minutes on short notice, but preparing for a title fight in less than a week took its toll. I was exhausted after going twenty-five minutes, tired from cutting twenty pounds on short notice, flying halfway across the world, and going from the couch to the cage in six days. As the fight was happening, all I could think was *This guy has no power.* Give me a proper eight-week camp and I could beat him. It was a double-edged sword because I didn't get the chance to showcase my best. I had fought on short notice with one hand tied behind my back. Part of me was thinking that I should have just taken less money and fought Usman with a proper eight-week camp from the start. Then maybe I would have had the belt and could ask for more money. Instead, I chose to fight for the best deal. No excuses.

Before we left the cage, I told Usman that I wanted a rematch. I couldn't take anything away from him: he had won the first one. But I was stubborn. I wanted that fucking belt because I knew I was better. I wanted to prove it in a rematch with a full eight weeks to prepare.

The UFC decided to give Usman a fight against Gilbert Burns in February 2021. All signs pointed to me getting the next title shot in the fall. I was a walking Evel Knievel, my body all fucking busted up from head to toe. Thinking I had some time to recover, I signed up to travel to Colombia to get stem cell treatment on my knees and wrists. I gave the UFC my itinerary and told them I'd be out of commission for a while. After the second day of procedures, I was stuck in a wheelchair, unable to walk, when the UFC called with a fight offer. "Fucking sweet. When?" I asked, assuming they meant in the fall. No. The fight, a rematch against Usman, was just four weeks away. "Listen, we know you're not ready," they said. "But you're gonna be the first event back to full capacity." For twelve months the UFC had been slowly working back from canceled fights to Fight Island to limited-capacity events. This was going to be the main event in Jacksonville in front of 15,000 fans. *Go fuck yourselves*, I thought. I was in a wheelchair and now they called me? I thought it was bullshit, calling me when I was crippled in Colombia after promising a fall fight. I told them it wasn't going to happen and hung up. But the next day I started using crutches and thought, *If I almost beat him on six days' notice, I could win in a month.*

I went against the doctor's advice and took the short-notice fight. The doc had told me I needed three to four weeks minimum before any serious training like weight lifting, running, or getting kicked in the fucking knee. I had one week where I couldn't do anything and then I got out of the wheelchair and started training. Outside of the stem cell treatment, I was in good shape because I had been training before the procedure; I just wasn't in *fight shape* to be ready in three weeks. But since I almost beat him in six days and felt his power and didn't think he could hurt me, I had thought, *Bro, sign me up.*

In the first fight, Usman hit me with some clean shots. I had been drained from the weight cut, so I worried going in that I might get KO'd early since your chin is weaker when you're dehydrated. But those punches didn't have power behind them and I lasted five rounds. I had no reason to worry in the rematch. And this time I only had to cut eight pounds instead of twenty, so I was feeling good going in. I thought it was all said and done.

But it ended up being the worst fucking night of my career. I took the short-notice fight and got knocked out—the first knockout loss of my life, and to a non-striker no less. It made no sense. Eight months before, I ate his punches for twenty-five minutes after a brutal weight cut. That entire fight I was telling myself, *This guy can never fucking hurt me. He can't punch through a wet paper bag.* Now suddenly he had the strongest punch I'd ever felt in my fucking life and put me out cold. He showed me something new and got my number. I was ready to wrestle for twenty-five minutes and he caught me by surprise. He won fair and square, so credit to him.

That KO loss was one of the sorest subjects of my career—another short-notice fight that ended in defeat. It ate at me because, while I felt like Usman was a great competitor, I thought I could've beaten him if I'd had a proper full camp. Other guys like Colby "Cupcake" Covington had six whole months to prep for their title bouts. But I only had six days the first time, then a month for the rematch. It made no sense why I felt that the UFC kept screwing me on prep time when I had been their top pay-per-view draw in back-to-back years. I was a much bigger draw than Colby ever was; the numbers proved it. His biggest selling PPV was, like, three hundred and something thousand compared to my 1.3 million. I just never understood why I didn't get the same full training camps as other guys.

Those short-notice title fights left a bad taste because I never got to showcase my best. I took gambles that backfired and paid the price. My bank account got fatter and my kids were set up for a better life because of those financial gains, but I had unfinished business. The losses ate me up inside because maybe if I had taken bad deals but gotten full camps, the story would have been different. Instead, I got beat on six days' notice and then knocked out on three weeks' notice. I was so close to realizing my destiny, I can't help but wonder if I would have a world champion belt had I had the proper preparation instead of rushed, last-minute training. The short-notice fights may have left scars, but they're part of my journey. I've learned that the bitter moments—the ones that made me think, *What if?*—are just as important to my story as the greatest victories.

CHAPTER 17

ALWAYS PUNCH BACK

I first met Colby Covington midway through 2011 when he strolled into the American Top Team gym fresh out of college through a program intended to get amateur wrestlers into MMA. American Top Team was home to countless top UFC fighters, along with world champion boxers and kickboxers, but Covington was recruited to the gym by Dan Lambert, who wanted to bolster the gym's wrestling talent.

I'd been training at ATT for nearly five years by then, grinding my way up the Strikeforce ranks and hovering on the verge of debuting in the UFC. Colby was just a twenty-three-year-old kid fresh out of Oregon State when he joined the team. When he first stepped foot in the gym, he looked like a fish out of water. But he could wrestle like hell and we both wanted the same thing. I needed to improve my wrestling defense and Colby wanted to learn how to strike, so we started working together during sessions. I taught him some nasty combinations and he worked with me on the mat for hours. We were training partners, but over time we became friends outside the gym too. We started running into each other at Seminole Casino Coconut Creek or Isle Casino Racing Pompano Park, where we both played poker after practice.

Pretty quickly I decided to introduce Colby to my striking coach, Paulino. "Look, this kid has a lot of potential," I told Paulino. Paulino was the best striking mind in the game and I knew he could take Colby's hands to the next level if he worked with him. So they started doing work together as Colby prepped for his first pro fight in 2012.

After a hot start to his career, Colby hit a rough patch in 2016. He was coming off his first career loss and trying to rebuild momentum to make a name for himself in the UFC. But he broke his hand, which sidelined him for months, and on top of that, I think that his girlfriend may even have dumped him around the same time. He had gotten kicked out of the team dorms at ATT for being a slob and didn't have the money for his own apartment, so the breakup left him with no place to live. I was an established pro fighter making decent money after completing forty-plus fights by then. I had my own place and some cash in the bank. Colby was in a bad spot with nowhere to go, so I took him in for a while and let him stay at my apartment so he could get back on his feet. He ended up crashing at my apartment for about nine months. We were cool: I did my thing and he did his. We didn't hang out much at the place, but we saw each other enough in the gym and poker rooms. If someone told me then that years later he would stab me in the back and become my enemy, I never would've believed it.

When I set Colby up with Paulino, they made a simple handshake deal: Paulino would train Colby in exchange for 5 percent of his fight earnings, no contracts. Same arrangement I had with Paulino my whole career. The two shook on it and had a gentleman's agreement. All Paulino ever asked for was 5 percent of whatever he made from fight earnings. If Colby made $100 and gave Paulino $5, cool. Over the next several years Paulino trained and cornered Colby as he climbed the UFC ranks. Colby earned his first title shot in 2018, a bout for the interim belt against Rafael dos Anjos at UFC 225 in June. That fight was what Colby and Paulino had been working toward, ever since I introduced the two to each other. I was right there in Chicago, cornering and celebrating with them, when Colby won the interim belt against dos Anjos. It was his biggest payout yet, around $350,000 total. But when it came time to pay Paulino his 5 percent cut, over $17,000, Colby ghosted him. I don't think he paid him a dime. From that moment on, I knew the guy was a piece of shit. I didn't want him around me. I wanted to take a fucking baseball bat and break it on his head, but my coach cooled me down, said we'd end up fighting in the cage one day and I could beat on him, get paid for it, and not go to jail.

For weeks I asked Colby why he hadn't given Paulino his money, and he either avoided the conversation or didn't give a straight answer. Paulino is like a father to me; he guided my whole career. He's the dude who took me from a hostile environment, realized my talent, and helped me get out of the fucking mess I was in. I ended up covering Paulino out of my pocket because I felt responsible for the introduction. That's when the relationship went sour. From that point on, Colby was dead to me.

A WAR OF WORDS

Things escalated quickly with Covington after I got back stateside from the Dominican Republic. I opened 2019 by knocking out Till and Askren back-to-back and suddenly I wasn't just another fighter: I was one of the biggest stars in the UFC. Meanwhile, Colby got into a contract dispute with the UFC after he beat dos Anjos and disappeared from the scene until he eventually took down Robbie Lawler in August 2019. We were both on the cusp of that welterweight title shot.

But fame and money had done something ugly to Colby. He always had a big mouth, but now he was shitting on his teammates for attention. After he beat Demian Maia in 2017, he bashed an entire country and its people. "Brazil, you're a dump!" he shouted to the crowd. "All you filthy animals suck." Half the gym was Brazilian, but that didn't stop him. Brazilian fighters in the gym refused to train with him. And it only got worse as he started to get more attention for his bullshit. He transformed the women's locker room into some video shoot, pissing off Joanna Jedrzejczyk. She gave him a piece of her mind and he got pissed. Then he tried to stir more shit up, predicting Khabib Nurmagomedov would beat our American Top Team teammate Dustin Poirier. The guy went full heel for some fucking Instagram and Twitter likes. The dude was just asking for trouble. Between stirring shit with teammates and stiffing Paulino, I was fucking done with him.

I was sitting behind Colby at UFC 241 in Anaheim—the same card when Diaz called me out for the BMF fight—and I tapped him on the shoulder, ready to man up. "What's all that shit talking, bro?" I asked him. "We're both men. You've got my number. Why don't we go outside and just talk like men?" He acted tough and called me unprofessional. They moved my seat to avoid a fight: Colby was and still is a straight coward outside the cage.

Things got worse when the UFC offered me Colby's title shot against Usman later that year after they couldn't reach a deal with him. Just hearing that I might take his place got under his skin. He started spewing shit like a broken sewer pipe. "I know you're dumb and desperate, but you spelled JOURNEYMAN TITLE wrong junior. Reading is fundamental and #supernecessary. Just like WINNING is #supernecessary to get title fights. You should try both sometime, you trash bag," he tweeted. And in the media, he was on ESPN, calling me jealous and bitter. Talk all you want, Colby, but do it to my face. I confronted him about the shit talk one day when I walked into ATT and saw him across the gym. I told him we needed to talk after practice. When he asked what it was about, I was straight-up: "You're being a bitch," I said. As I turned to walk away, he screamed for all to hear, "I'll fucking kill you, bro. Don't ever talk to me like that." The whole gym stopped. Coaches and teammates had to separate us. After that, they started changing Colby's training schedule to keep us apart. This clown used to sleep on my couch but now he couldn't be in the same room as me. Whenever I walked into the gym, he ran out the back door. Spineless.

Everybody thinks MMA is an individual sport—two guys in a cage fighting—and it is, three nights a year. The other 362 days it's a fucking team sport. You need everybody together, training, making each other better. What I felt was that Colby's toxicity seemed to be tearing American Top Team apart from the inside. So in March 2020, Dan instituted a zero-tolerance policy: No ATT fighters could talk trash about teammates unless they had a fight agreement. Dan sat me and Colby down to tell us. "You guys are ruining the mojo of our gym. You're ruining our environment here. Nobody's bigger than our gym," he said. "If you guys do this again, you're both out." I wasn't having any of it. Colby had done all this shit talking, blasted everyone in the gym, and now they were putting this gag order in place just to protect Colby after, in my mind, he threw the whole gym under the bus? I don't do well with ultimatums. I took to Twitter and called Colby out. "Fuck [Colby]. The most fragile most sensitive guy in UFC history. Can't kick me out cause this rule was for fighters only. Not crotch sniffers that get their jaw broken by other crotch sniffers. @AmericanTopTeam we all know that dude is no fighter."

Almost immediately, my phone buzzed. It was a group text from Dan, addressed to me and Colby. "I liked you guys a hell of a lot better when you were broke as shit and cared about the team instead of just yourselves," Dan wrote. "Fuck off. Neither one of you is welcome back to the gym. I hope you end up fighting each other and beating the living shit out of each other."

I thought Dan was trolling me. Colby texted back that he

understood. I called Dan right away. "Fuck you, dude. You ain't kicking me out of that gym," I said. "I've been there as long as you have, motherfucker. I'm next in line when you and Richie die to take over that gym. I'm not going anywhere."

Dan didn't budge.

"Dude, nothing personal," he said. "I gotta do it."

"No, you can't kick me out," I said. "Fuck you!"

"I'm serious," he said, not relenting. "I love you, we can go to dinner, hang out anytime you want, but you can't come back."

I told him I would be at the gym the next day. Dan was having none of it. "Dude, you can't go back to the gym." *Click.*

One week went by and that week turned into a month, and then two months, and then three months. Every week or so I'd call Dan and the conversation was always the same.

"Hey, motherfucker," I'd say. "I'm coming back. I'm gonna fucking run you over, bro. I'm gonna take my car and take your knees out, bro, if you don't let me back in the gym."

"Don't come back, Jorge," Dan would warn.

For several months I stayed away, training in Miami with Paulino and Coach Brown. After three months I knew I had to pull out the big guns. I started texting Dan's kids, who I had grown close with over the years. One day Dan sent them a text for dinner plans and my plan started to work.

"Hey, guys, what's going on?" Dan asked his kids in a group message. "You guys want to hit Chima tonight?"

His daughter texted back.

"Sorry, Dad," she said. "I promised Jorge I wouldn't talk to you until you brought him back to the gym."

The texts from the other kids followed.

"Me too," they all said.

I remember Dan calling me.

CHAPTER 18

FIGHTING FOR TRUTH

Growing up, if you asked me, *What's the greatest country?* I would have shouted, *America!* But when I was young, there was no American Dream by any stretch. Growing up broke in Miami, I felt my family had been fooled by false advertising. The "American Dream" sounded more like a fairy tale.

From as early as I can remember, every Sunday my family would gather around the table and recount horror stories about how bad Cuba and communism were. I was in awe hearing the story of how my father and his family had lived through the violent Cuban Revolution and finally escaped, choosing to sail blindly on the tractor tire toward Florida even if it killed him because staying wasn't an option. America was the last grasp of hope and freedom. My aunt had risked running through a minefield just to escape, a fact I could hardly believe. But while they went on and on at dinner about America's endless possibilities, I only saw our dirty reality: my Cuban immigrant family was broke and I was cutting fucking grass as we struggled to get by. I had been *this close* to being in the system. As a kid, I felt more like a second-class citizen questioning what was so great about this country.

America seemed like a strange place where the rich could practically get away with murder while kids like me were on the verge of being swallowed by the system for every little wrongdoing. In my mind, you had to be born into success.

I first came across Donald Trump while watching boxing. He was always hosting boxing matches at the Trump Taj Mahal in Atlantic City. Later, he helped give the UFC its first big break. When many people wouldn't touch the sport because of liabilities, Trump allowed the UFC to hold fights in Atlantic City and all of his other casinos and venues around the country, helping MMA gain mainstream acceptance. As a kid, all I knew was that Trump was big in the fighting world and owned the Miss Universe pageant. I didn't know anyone could *own* that thing. I thought that was the coolest shit ever. When I was twenty-something, I saw Trump become a reality star on *The Apprentice*, shouting, "You're fired!" I was a huge Trump fan. The public perception was that Trump was an asshole, but, damn it, I loved him. He seemed the brash dude I'd be if I ever had money. There was just something about his swagger even then.

In my mind, Trump was the definition of success, but it wasn't just boxing matches, casinos, or Miss Universe that caught my attention. I watched Trump's documentary after I found out who he was and realized his story wasn't one of success at every turn in life. He had failed, declared bankruptcy multiple times, and come back stronger every time. He always reinvented himself and saw what he had to do to move forward. Seeing how he had made it big even after high-profile bankruptcies inspired me. If this guy could start with everything, fail over and over, and claw his way back, maybe the American Dream was possible. My whole life I had been handed losses, but every time I learned from them and got better. I realized the key to success was not letting the fear of missing stop you from swinging.

Maybe the United States did hold the keys. To win, you just had to grab life by the throat and squeeze like Trump did. I started to believe the American Dream just might be real if you were determined enough to take it. You just have to have the idea, the fortitude, and the direction.

THE POLITICAL ARENA

In 2019, I fought three times, and every time, my social media blew the hell up. My following doubled or tripled with each fight. I never thought I had a voice, but suddenly I had a platform. I wasn't sure if people were going to love it or hate it, but I didn't give a fuck. I wasn't about to pretend to be someone I wasn't. I was going to shoot from the heart, something I had done since I was a kid. As I watched the chaos in the United States escalate during COVID, I decided enough was enough. It was time to fucking speak my mind.

I always admired Muhammad Ali, not just for his fighting, but for standing up against war and for human rights. He sat out the prime of his career, for three years, all because of his beliefs. To me, the man was unmovable. I thought, *That's how I need to be. Just be me.* I knew opening my mouth was like shooting myself in the foot. I'd probably lose sponsors, piss people off, limit my following. But fuck it. This is the greatest country in the world because of the Constitution and the values it holds. I had to speak my mind and stand up for what I believed in.

Everyone was telling me to stick to fighting. Just shut up and throw punches. Except for Papa Dukes. If I mentioned losing sponsors, he'd say something like *If we lose the country, that money doesn't matter.* We grew up hating and knowing the evil of communism and knew that if it ever came knocking, we had to fight it with everything we had. For the longest time, I thought my dad was paranoid. But then the years before and after Trump happened and I saw he was on point. If it wasn't for Trump, who knows how messed up things could've gotten?

I started posting videos on YouTube in 2020, and suddenly I was getting demonetized, shadow banned, and suspended. Videos that used to bring in views and cash were getting flagged left and right. Most of the videos weren't even political, but before I knew it, I had too many violations and my account was shut down. They even took down a video with 50 million views because it got too much traction. You-Tube put the hammer down. Talking about Trump, I didn't care if every sponsor dropped me. I believed in one thing with all my heart: Trump stands for freedom. He stands for me, for you, for we the people. I'd be damned if I didn't stand up for what I believe in; screw the consequences.

After Trump attended the BMF fight in New York, our relationship picked up. Officially, I can't tell you about the first time I met him: it's classified. But I can tell you about the second time. During his reelection campaign in 2020, I decided to show my support at Trump National Doral Golf Club in Miami. I was in the crowd, three or four rows deep, and he called me out from the podium. I didn't know it was coming. I was at the rally to show my support because I fucking loved the guy. He had to say my name a few times because I didn't realize he was talking to me. Someone elbowed me to get my attention and I acknowledged him. "Hey, Mr. President, I'm right here," I said, surprised as hell.

The next time President Trump came to Miami, his people asked me to meet him at the airport. So there I was, waiting on the runway with the mayor of Miami. It was the middle of COVID, so everyone was masked up. I still remember a lady running around and giving me instructions. "Under no conditions will you make contact with the president," she told me who knows how many times. "Do not reach your hand out; he will not shake it." Air Force One landed and there he was, the Donald himself. He walked toward us, gave the mayor a nod, and then walked straight to me and put his hand out for a fist bump. I'm thinking, *Are you fucking kidding me? Bop!* I pounded the fucking shit out of his hand. He invited me to the town hall and went off to his car. The cameras turned off and the woman started flipping out. "Was I gonna leave the president hanging?" I asked her.

I'm Trump's favorite fighter. It's bananas. He'd call me six weeks before a fight and the day of weigh-ins. He would leave voicemails when I didn't answer. "Hey, I'll be watching you. Do your thing. When you're at your best, you are the best." It's mind-blowing that the guy I looked up to the most would give me words of encouragement.

Trump's not everyone's cup of tea and neither am I. That's cool. But to those who vibe with me, they see a God-fearing man who fuck-ing loves this country, who busted his ass for everything, and is as real as they come. That pisses some people off. I won't change or pander. I stand for what I believe in, no matter the heat.

MY PLATFORM TO SPEAK

Sitting around the table on Sundays with my family, I never thought I'd be talking politics. But life has a way of pulling you into unexpected bat-tles. Some people might think a fighter should stick to what he knows, but the truth is we're not just fighters. We're citizens, immigrants, sons, fathers.

I've been on the journey to the American Dream since I was a kid riding my bike through the streets of Miami. As the son of immigrant parents who has big dreams, I hustled for every opportunity. I've faced discrimination in my life, been shoved to the ground by cops, and had my face on the concrete for doing nothing. I've been discriminated against more than you'd believe just because I have a tattoo on my neck and I'm a Latin dude. I wasn't always Jorge "Gamebred" Masvidal. For most of my life, nobody knew me from any other South Florida immigrant. And now people throw labels at me based on who or what I support politically. Society now puts you in a box. If you're for Trump or a Republican, suddenly you hate everything. If you're a Democrat, they say you're Antifa. It's like if you're not with one side, you're the enemy. There's no middle ground. The divide-and-conquer tactics straight out of Cuba's playbook are now being used here. What the hell is this country coming to?

I've been slapped with the racist label for supporting Trump. People shout, "Racism!" conveniently forgetting all the good Trump did for minority communities like mine. The lowest unemployment rates for Latin and Black people. But people blame everything on race when there are real issues that can be addressed and fixed. I know about racism. I also know about the failures of communism and socialism from the pain and sacrifice my family endured escaping Castro's Cuba. So when I see the far-left direction this country is drifting toward, I get worried. I'd rather listen to the oldest person in the room who survived communism or socialism firsthand over some punk just out of college who hasn't experienced life but has a theory. Freedom and capitalism are what made immigrants risk their lives to escape to America. In my opinion, strong borders and fair immigration maintain that.

Immigration is one of the things that makes America great. I wouldn't be here if it wasn't for the United States welcoming people like me from other countries and cultures with open arms. Fuck, immigrants built this country. But I feel immigration has to be done in a regulated way. Everybody has to follow laws. My mom had to get permission to come to the United States from Peru and my dad eventually got permission after he escaped Cuba and touched ground on American soil. This is a nation of laws, and everyone, including my mom and dad, had to follow them to get here. Every person, regardless of where they come from, deserves to be treated with dignity and respect throughout the process. And if someone arrives in America from somewhere like Cuba, Venezuela, Haiti, or Brazil—somewhere where they're fleeing death or persecution—we shouldn't just throw them back. But we can't have open borders either. Get in, but at a rate the country can handle. I think that Trump's approach was working. Latino unemployment was at its lowest during his term. Do it right, get your paperwork, work, and pay taxes. There has to be a process to manage the influx based on jobs available and people we can absorb. When someone skips the line or hides in the shadows without paperwork, it's unsustainable.

I'm not anti-immigrant. But this is the greatest country in the world and we can't risk compromising that. Unregulated immigration leads to mass shootings, bombings, drug trafficking, and sex trafficking. I want my kids to grow up with the same American ideals my parents dreamed about and came here for, not with failed systems and violence invading from abroad. I feel for immigrants, but once someone is here, they should remember why they came: because it's the greatest country in the world. Don't bring the bullshit from back home. This is the greatest country for a reason: the United States Constitution. We don't need nobody else's constitution. If it was going on over there, leave it there. Look at countries like Venezuela, once the richest country in South America, now broke due to bad policies and government mismanagement.

My family fled Cuba's communist regime for the American ideal, capitalism and democracy. My family, like so many others, left their country for the capitalism of the United States. I defend capitalism and American democracy because my family has seen the alternative. Just ask Cubans and Venezuelans escaping authoritarian regimes why they fled here: because socialism and communism can destroy the quality of life. Papa Dukes and so many others like him made the sacrifice to abandon everything they knew for America because they didn't want to be told what to do. They wanted the hustle, the grind, and the rewards for chasing their dreams. Now I see that ideal in danger under regressive policies threatening to extinguish everything special about the American Dream. It's like some extreme politicians want to take what people earn and hand out participation trophies instead of letting people earn their keep. We can't let the land of the free turn into a place where handouts replace hard work. We've got to defend what made this country a dream for immigrants: the chance to earn their place and create your dream, not dictators calling all the shots and giving handouts.

When you force companies overseas through crippling regulations and suffocating taxes, real working families suffer. Mama Dukes, bless her soul, worked multiple jobs just to keep the lights on and food on the table. Politicians like Obama, Biden, and, yeah, even some Republicans betrayed citizens to line their own pockets. They're cozying up to China, sending manufacturing jobs packing overseas, and leaving us to pick up the pieces. When Trump was running the show, the United States was a force to be reckoned with. America was strong and the world respected and feared us. There was no talk of new wars. But now, under these new policies, they're tossing trillions into the war machine while our cities are falling apart. Every time we go to war, somebody gets rich. Maybe it's not you or me, but somebody out there is getting rich. It's a fucking shame. They feed us this line about caring for the everyday person, but it's all a load of bullshit. I want an America-first mentality when it comes to trade, taxes, and security; they should be helping Americans, not selling them out to some globalist agenda.

I don't claim to be an expert on politics or policy. But I have strong views when it comes to freedom, the economy, immigration, and things that impact people like me. I've heard the stories of people who left their homes for a better life in America and have seen some of it firsthand. That's where my views come from—not some fake wokeness. I've seen signs from today's politicians of what my Cuban family warned me about and now I have the platform to be a voice of opposition. We need real leaders ready to take the country in the right direction for all people. And we need citizens who can think for themselves instead of just choosing sides and canceling anyone who disagrees. I'm ready for that conversation.

I say with all my heart: Give me freedom or give me death. If you don't believe in those words, you're the problem with society.

CHAPTER 19

HOMECOMING

I was buzzing with excitement and adrenaline as John Wallace and I walked out of American Airlines Arena toward the bar following UFC 42, the first-ever UFC event in Miami. It was 2003, and after years of streaming pay-per-views at friends' houses, seeing legends like Matt Hughes fight before my eyes was surreal. These were the fighters I had worshipped. But as we walked down the Miami sidewalk, I went from being starstruck to being certain of my future: I could be in there with them one day. That night I decided I was going to be in that cage one day, bringing a UFC event back to my city.

But first I had a grappling competition the next morning. The only problem? By the time we got to the train station just after midnight, we had missed the last train home. Neither of us had a cent left to our names. The next train didn't leave until sunrise, so with nobody to come pick us up and no money for a cab, we opted to just sleep under a bench at the train station. Not to sound like a tough guy, but it wasn't my first time catching Zs on hard concrete. I was eighteen and I'd already done a night in jail by then and slept on cold concrete using sandals as a pillow. Not to mention, me and Mama

Dukes were always on the move, so I was used to sleeping in uncomfortable places.

We slept under the benches until the first trains rumbled to life around 5 a.m. *Boom*, I woke up, rode the train home, changed clothes, then hopped on one of my beat-up bikes. Since I was a little kid I have always relied on my bikes to get me where I needed. My bike took me wherever the fuck I wanted to go. I had countless bikes growing up. One that Mama Dukes had bought got jacked when I was eleven or so and it destroyed me. Whether it was $20 or $200, I knew she had worked her ass off for it. I was young and full of rage. I didn't know who stole the bike, so I vented my anger out by stealing a few bikes in the neighborhood. Me and my friends would slap on pegs so someone else could ride on the front, back, or both. That morning I picked a bike and hauled ass across town, half-dead from no sleep but running on adrenaline after watching UFC 42.

I met my friends at the gym and we loaded up for the North American Grappling Association tournament. I competed in two divisions—won one and placed in another. A few weeks later I fought in my first pro MMA bout in Fort Lauderdale.

That was the start of twenty long years on the road, fighting other fighters in their backyard, on their home turf. I would spend countless hours on flights to other cities, sleeping in hotels, and fighting in front of hostile crowds. I didn't know then how long it would take, the ups and downs I'd face, or the scars I'd get along the way, but from that night in 2003, I was obsessed with realizing my dream to fight in Miami. Whatever it took.

BACK TO THE 305

For years the UFC had asked me to headline an event in Miami, where my fighting dreams began. The call of home made it hard, but I always refused. It was ironic considering how much I had always wanted to fight in my backyard.

That was before I truly understood the toll of fighting at the highest level. I'd faced opponents in their hometowns and witnessed the stress and pressure it put on a fighter. Picture this: everyone and their mother, who barely knew you but has maybe heard of you, suddenly wants tickets. I went to school in Miami. Fuck, I went to *a lot* of schools in Miami. And in every one of those schools, there was a bus driver who drove me to school. That bus driver had a kid, and that kid had a cousin, and now everyone and their mother wanted a piece of the action. It's a lot of pressure. More media commitments, more demands to be here, there, and everywhere. It's worth it in some ways, but at the same time it's not. With the UFC, you don't get a cut from the gate; it's all flat fees. Fast-forward a bit, and I ended up with the highest-grossing gate at American Airlines Arena, surpassing even LeBron James winning championships for the Heat. We raked in $14 million from the gate. Wanna know how much I saw from that? Fucking zero. So, as you think of returning home, you start to question: Why put yourself through all that?

In early 2023, after saying no countless times, I finally agreed to fight Gilbert Burns in Miami at UFC 287. The second loss to Usman, the only knockout I'd ever suffered in my career, served as a wake-up call. I could sense that my reflexes weren't what they used to be. It's different if you get knocked out early on; you have time to recover. But late in your career, it changes the game. After that fight, I started feeling mortal. Don't get me wrong: I still believed I could take on and beat plenty of the mid-tier guys, but that wasn't what I'd signed up for. I was in it to face the absolute best of the best. I didn't dedicate my life to this sport just to be average.

I decided it was time for a gut check. Miami was where it all started for me—where I had trained, where I had taken off. Now, two decades later, I found myself at a crossroads. It was either time for a rebirth of my career, another monumental run, or time to call it quits and ride off into the sunset on my turf. If I lost to Burns, there would be no denying it: I had no business competing at this level anymore.

Outsiders might look at MMA and see it as two guys swinging and kicking as hard as they can, beating the shit out of each other. But there's a whole lot more to it than meets the eye. When I'm launching a punch at someone, my brain is processing a million things: how they're moving, the distance, whether the punch is going to curve or turn into a hook. In the UFC, I was going up against the world's best athletes and fighters. If you're a millisecond off, you could get KO'd or caught in a submission. You've got to see the depths, assess the timing of that depth, process a ton of energy, and be aware of all the sensors. If I throw a punch and miss, I'm exposed, and the other guy can capitalize. It's a constant dance of waiting for the right time to strike while not letting the fear of missing stop you from swinging. It's a high-stakes game of chess and every move matters. That data used to flow seamlessly early in my career, but by year twenty I felt like it had slowed down dramatically. All of a sudden I was getting hit and eating punches. I could see them coming, but my body wasn't reacting the way it used to.

In the gym, I felt like I was on top of the world, performing phenomenally against the best. But what happens in the gym, even against the best, isn't fight speed. I had doubts about whether I still had that connection from the brain to the body, the split-second decision-making that defines success in the cage. The decision to fight in Miami wasn't just about the outcome; it was about the actual performance.

Part of me considered it a judgment match. I knew my speed, power, and strength had dwindled in certain areas. It was more about the performance, showcasing whether I still had what it took. Retirement wasn't set in stone, but I was laying it all on the line in Miami.

The outcome would determine not just the end of a fight but possibly the end of an era.

LEAVING THE OCTAGON BEHIND

Fighting in Miami almost felt like cheating, a hometown advantage I'd never experienced before. No flights, no hotels. I was sleeping in my bed and driving my car to the arena. It was a different vibe, a different feeling.

The day of the fight, I woke up in my bed surrounded by everything I'd ever wanted on fight day: my son, my trainers, the cold plunge. The sleep I got the night before the fight was the best I'd ever had. I closed my eyes the evening before and when I opened them it was 7:30 a.m. on fight day. No tossing and turning, no waking up in the middle of the night. No travel fatigue or distractions. After my normal training, I did specialized hand-eye coordination drills and meditation, things I didn't normally get to do on the days of my fights. It was all falling into place. I had no excuses. It was the best version of me.

If there wasn't already enough hype around the fight and my homecoming to the 305, President Trump called me a few weeks out before the fight to tell me he'd be there. The greatest president in the world, in the middle of going through allegations about the election, took the time to send me messages. He said, "Hey, six weeks out Masvidal, hope everything is going well. Stay focused." Three weeks later he said, "Hey, how's training going? I hope you're good." For him to make time during his legal battles to offer encouragement was surreal and humbling. Before the fight, they took me to a special room to meet with him, and he hyped me up. "You're the best in the world when you're on. Everybody's watching you," he said. "The whole country's watching."

It was time to roll the dice. Standing in the Octagon almost twenty years after watching my first fight from the same stands was fucking crazy. The crowd chanted "305" as the first round started, and then a "Let's go, Jorge" chant emerged as we exchanged punches. But as the minutes ticked away, something wasn't right. My game plan, crafted in the gym, wasn't working. My timing and speed felt off, unable to pull the trigger. I kept trying to will things that flowed in camp but overcommitted, ending up on my back against Burns, the jujitsu world champion. By round two I knew my chances were fading. Entering the third round, I had to dig deep, go for broke, and secure the victory. I left my corner ready to empty the tank. But despite my efforts to claim a hometown victory, I kept coming up short. It felt like, maybe at this stage, I didn't have it anymore. Burns took me down to secure the *W*.

The realization hit hard: I couldn't win in front of my president, in front of my city. It was painful. There were no injuries, no visible wounds, just the loss of that spark that pushes you to the next level. In my heart, I believed that if I had fought this guy two years earlier, I would have knocked him out in the first round. He made mistakes that I saw in real time but I couldn't capitalize on them. There's a magic to fighting, and on that night I just didn't have it. That transfer of data from body to head and back was no longer there. Even if I had given Burns the finish I wanted to give him in Miami and knocked him out with ten seconds to go, I would still have retired. My performance until that moment wasn't at the elite level. I wasn't there to be a stepping stone for other fighters. I always said that once the sport passed me by, I'd gracefully bow out.

I was at the pinnacle of my career in popularity, so it fucking sucked to admit that I no longer had that MMA grittiness. I could have taken fights against top-ten opponents or guys outside the rankings, but I signed up for the sport to face the best available. I never wanted to continue past the point where it wasn't fun. It wasn't a planned decision.

At that moment, surrounded by a cheering crowd, I felt sick. I hadn't given them what they deserved. I didn't have it in me at that level anymore. That's when it hit me: *What better place to call it quits than where it all began?* This city, my city, had shown me unwavering support time and time again. As the final seconds ticked away in a three-round loss, I made the decision: I was done. I took off my gloves and embraced my son and daughter.

The speech was unplanned and unprepared. When Joe Rogan put the microphone up to my face, I spoke from my heart.

"I love everybody here, thanks for watching. But this is where I started my career, it's been a long twenty years, fifty-something fights. Sometimes your favorite basketball player doesn't have that 3-pointer no more. Your favorite quarterback loses that rifle. I don't feel the same when I get in here no more. It's been twenty long years. I love all of you. The UFC came here twenty years ago, and it inspired me to chase this dream for twenty years. Fifty-something fights later hopefully I inspired somebody in here to fight for theirs, no matter what it is. If it's in the sports world, if it's in the fucking entertainment world, if it's in whatever world. The 9-to-5. I love everybody. I love this sport. I'm a multimillionaire. I didn't have shit when I started. I can say I'm set for life now. I love you guys, man."

I gave a shout-out to my president and walked out of the cage. President Trump and I developed a great relationship during my career. He was always cheering me on and motivating me with texts and calls and attending fights and I was out supporting him in Florida every chance I got. After he attended my last fight in the cage, he texted me: "Jorge, thanks for being there and always being with me. You are special and so respected in our community and far beyond."

There were fans in the stands crying. It wasn't the ending I had hoped for. I wanted everyone to be happy, not crying. But I understood the emotion: I had been everyone's favorite fighter for a long time, and now I was hanging it up. As I walked out of the cage, my son on my shoulders, the cheers of the 305 gave me chills. Nothing mattered more to me at that moment than being with my daughter and son—the driving force behind this entire journey. My daughter, especially, had been there since we had nothing, living in a cramped one-bedroom, five-hundred-square-foot apartment—kitchen, bathroom, everything combined. She experienced a life where she went to school with the same shoes and clothes, the little materialistic things kids notice. She didn't have nice lunches and her dad didn't have a nice car, let alone a house. Those were the circumstances she grew up with. Then, overnight, everything changed. I was so happy she could share this moment with me, having been there for the entire ride. She saw firsthand that you can do anything in this world that you put your mind to.

The average time span of a UFC career is four years. I got ten. The typical professional fighter's career lasts maybe a decade. Mine spanned two. I always knew I was born to fight, not just in the cage, but in the face of everything standing in my way. I achieved what I had set out to do. From "Street Jesus" fighting in backyard brawls to "Gamebred" headlining arenas across the world, I fought to beat the odds and set an example coming from nothing, punching back against circumstances saying I couldn't. Not many banked on me becoming a pay-per-view seller and a household name when I started swinging in Kimbo's backyards. Even I doubted after setbacks. But betting on myself and getting off the mat after every blow made me who I was. I like to think Miami supported me, not just because I won or lost a fight, but because they saw a piece of themselves in my journey. If a kid from the streets of Miami, with all the odds stacked against him, could make it to the top of the fighting world, then they could beat whatever challenges life threw their way.

CHAPTER 20

LEGACY

I drove straight home after I left American Airlines Arena, twenty years of the ride of my life flashing before me. Where the fuck did the time go? One minute I was a skinny eighteen-year-old street kid hungry to prove himself. The next I was a thirty-eight-year-old veteran staring down the road of retirement. There was no easing into my new reality. That shit was fucking real.

I woke up the next morning in my bed for the first time in my career without a fight to prepare for. It was fucking weird. What was next? I can't tell you how many fucking people asked me that question. I didn't have a clue. My only plan was not to have one. For the first time in over twenty years there was no fight to negotiate, no fighter to game plan, no endless grind of hitting the gym two or three times a day, five or six days a week. Twenty years and fifty-two fights, from age eighteen to thirty-eight, took its toll. I just needed a break from that nonstop cycle I'd been on for over half my life. For once there was no next opponent, no film to study, no strategy to map out. The never-ending routine I'd built my life around had slammed to a halt overnight.

I learned so much from every fight—about myself, about fighting, about life. In my world, life is full of instant gratification. Win a fight and your phone blows up with 1,000 messages. Lose and you might get fifty texts. *Maybe.* I learned fast that my feelings and emotions couldn't be dependent on the opinions of others. My emotions were my responsibility alone. Everyone has an opinion, but at the end of the day, you have to trust yourself first. To be successful, you need to be happy upstairs.

Navigating to the top was a lonely road. I ditched friends who didn't understand the obsessive focus required to be the best or those who I thought would only drag me down a dark path. As I got deeper into my career, I had to leave behind friends I grew up with, dudes who had been with me through the kind of shit that bonds you for life, or so I thought. Eventually, I reached a tipping point. I could keep running the streets and end up like Papa Dukes in prison. Or I could grind in the gym and make something of myself. My dad warned me that a lot of people don't deserve to be in your corner. He never really liked any friend I ever had. He knew I was easily in-fluenced by those closest to me and he trusted almost no one around me. As their rap sheets grew, I cut ties. It killed me to tell dudes I loved that we couldn't kick it anymore. But the lure of fast money and bad decisions was too strong for both them and me. So I left people I cared about behind. Some of those people ended up behind bars, others dead.

When I busted up my hand, I got weak and reached out to some of them to help me make quick cash. I couldn't afford to be out of work and thought they could guide me without getting my hands dirty. Luckily, I realized before it was too late that their brand of help would only land me behind bars or in the ground. Part of me wonders if that would have been my fate, too, if a call back to the cage hadn't put me back on the better path—the road that led me to the Octagon instead of a concrete cell.

Real friends are hard to find in this world. I've had coaches betray me over the years. Dudes I looked up to until they said shit to tear me down instead of building me up. But out of all those people, I found Paulino. Win or lose, he kept it real on what I needed to improve. He cared, and that's all I ever needed. Ride-or-die people like that are hard to find. That support from guys like Paulino and Coach Brown made all the difference. A few key people believing in you and your potential can carry you a long way. It makes you believe in yourself.

I can't help but think I should have won a title belt or two if only I had woken up faster to the bad influences around me. If I had been less stubborn and more focused. The truth is my stupidity in my early years kept me from reaching my full potential. It bothers me that I left something on the table. Hindsight may be 20/20, but time machines don't exist. That was all part of my journey to be the man I am today. Just as my thirty-five wins changed everything for me and my family, the mistakes along the way defined my path too. The past is done. But in the future we don't have to repeat old mistakes. Whatever I do going forward, whether in fighting, business, or whatever else life throws my way, I'll be prepared for all scenarios. I'll have plans A through Z laid out. The fight game schooled me in invaluable life lessons. Control what you can. Learn from falls along the way. Get up when life knocks you down. And keep fucking swinging.

GAMEBRED BAREKNUCKLE

My first taste of fighting came long before I slipped on padded gloves and stepped into the cage. It was throwing down in the rawest form:

bare-knuckle. Whether it was in the schoolyard or backyard brawls, throwing bare fists was the first form of fighting I ever knew. Raw and real from the jump. Long before coaches and strategy, I let my fists do the talking.

Backyard brawling is what first put me on the map. Kimbo Slice helped make fighters like me mainstream with his unsanctioned, bare-knuckle backyard brawls on YouTube. Millions of people watched, and from there my legend grew to what it became. Many of my most loyal fans throughout my career knew me as "Street Jesus" before I was ever "Gamebred." So when I started thinking about life after the Octagon, fate brought shit full circle.

During the COVID lockdown, I got an itch to do something in the promotion world and I wanted it to be different. Bare-knuckle fighting is the new wave, and it's fucking wild. It's as real as it gets: trained fighters throwing hands against one another with nothing but skin and bones. No gloves to soften blows. Land a clean blow and the fight changes in an instant. There are way more cuts and KOs. It's how the early UFC went down. As the sport evolved, they brought gloves and rules to cut down the violence. I'm taking it back to those roots with Gamebred. Just two bad motherfuckers looking to take each other out by any means necessary. I wanted to get back to the pure form of fighting that Kimbo's fights captured and combine it with the top talent and production of the MMA world I came up in. I called up my friend Dean Toole, who I knew from the promotion scene, and he was all in. That's how the idea of Gamebred Bare-knuckle MMA was born.

There are a lot of great promoters, but I'm not trying to be just another promoter churning out fights. I might not be able to bang at the highest level in MMA anymore, but I can still put on some of the best fights on planet Earth from the promoter's seat. I want to add twists that keep fans guessing and on the edge of their seats. Boxing versus

MMA. Bare-knuckle brawls. My goal is to shake up the fight game and become a top promoter in the process, using my connections and experience to make the fights people didn't even realize they wanted to see. I've worn almost every hat in the game, from fighter to corner-man to sparring partner to coach to manager. Promoting might be the best and most natural of the hats I've worn. The only thing I loved as much as fighting myself was the promoting side. Making fights happen and putting asses in seats. I want to give back to the next generation and help rising stars find the same spotlights I got to shine in thanks to people like Kimbo. That YouTube buzz he created made this sport blow up. I want to keep surprising fans and give dudes a platform to go viral themselves.

We launched Gamebred Bareknuckle MMA as a fully sanctioned MMA card without gloves in 2021. Within two years we had former UFC heavyweight champs Junior dos Santos and Fabricio Werdum as a main event in Vegas. It was surreal standing there as the CEO of my promotion as two former UFC champs weighed in. I'm not going to lie: I was a little fucking nervous. At the beginning, when this was just an idea, Dean and I would talk about names like those guys fighting for Gamebred, and now they were throwing down.

Gamebred is just getting warmed up. This is my passion. We want to bring the meanest guys in the world out to fight each other. I want to treat the fighters better than they're treated anywhere else. If we do it right, we're going to ride this fucker for a long time. They say if you do what you love, you never work a day in your life. And this doesn't feel like work.

I think Kimbo would be proud if he could see it. We came from similar paths and had to work extra hard to make it where we did. In many ways Gamebred Bareknuckle is trying to carry on the vision he started. If it wasn't my league, I think it would be Kimbo's. He made street fighters like me mainstream. Now I want to do the same thing, take the true art of fighting from the streets to arenas across the world. This new ride as a promoter feels like my career coming full circle.

THE FIGHT CONTINUES

When you're born to fight, it never truly leaves you. I said goodbye to the Octagon but I didn't say goodbye to fighting. The dog never left me. Sparring at the gym with the best—that shit is like pickup basketball to me. I love to fight and find out who's fucking better.

I think about competing again almost every night. In the gym I'll have flashes that make the coaches say, "You've still got it." I know my reactions have slowed and I can't absorb the same punishment anymore. MMA is a young man's game that won't see me again. But can I say I'm retired from fighting for life? Not a chance. Fighting has been my life. All I knew and did for twenty years, night and day, day and night, was fight. The habit is hard to break.

I'm still fighting, even if my days in the Octagon are behind me. None of the boxing guys have ever come to MMA and been successful; it just doesn't happen. Reflexes and sensory overload are on a whole different level in MMA compared to boxing. Boxing is just hands: jab, hook, uppercut to the face, and repeat. Six different attacks from each hand to the body and face. In MMA, you've got the knee, the elbow, the kick, the takedown, the clinch—a ton of options that demand your sensors to fire at a different speed. I may have lost a step in the cage, but going from the sensory overload of MMA to just using my hands in boxing? Now, that's in my wheelhouse. I want to carry the MMA flag into the ring against traditional boxers and show the fighting world what a well-rounded striker can do. Who knows what other twists or turns might unfold in my story? Wherever it goes, you best believe fists will lead the way.

People are always asking me about my legacy. They see a twenty-year MMA career in the rearview mirror and assume my best days are behind me. But the truth is, as I write this, I'm not even forty fucking years old yet. I've closed one door, but the story of Gamebred is far from over. It's just entering another round.

The fight continues.